Praise for David C. Banks, *SOAR*, and the Eagle Academies

"David Banks is not just an extraordinary educator, he's a great innovator. The Eagle Academy defied political correctness to do what was right for young men facing enormous challenges. It is a big idea that is saving lives and providing hope."

—Joel Klein, former chancellor of the New York City
Department of Education

"We've got to do more to give families the tools and the support that they should have so that they can be the best parents. They are a child's first teachers. I want to commend the 100 Black Men, because I worked with the 100 Black Men in New York to help create the Eagle Academy, a high school for young African-American and Latino men."

—Hillary Rodham Clinton, former New York senator
and secretary of state

"Eagle Academy is a model for improving student achievement."

—Michael Bloomberg, former mayor of New York

"How do we get young people off the bench and into the game? Strong, committed father figures, ready to train, prepare, coach, and mentor young people so they can grow into champions. Eagle Academy doesn't just teach academic skills, it models character, so that Eagle graduates can be successful men—the next generation of the men and fathers we need. David Banks shows us how to stand up and save our boys."

—Allan Houston, assistant general manager, New York Knicks

SOAR

HOW BOYS LEARN, SUCCEED, AND DEVELOP CHARACTER

DAVID C. BANKS
WITH G. F. LICHTENBERG

37 INK

—

ATRIA

NEW YORK   LONDON   TORONTO   SYDNEY   NEW DELHI

ATRIA PAPERBACK
An Imprint of Simon & Schuster, Inc.
1230 Avenue of the Americas
New York, NY 10020

First 37 INK/Atria Paperback edition April 2015

37 INK / ATRIA PAPERBACK and colophons are trademarks of Simon & Schuster, Inc.

For information about special discounts for bulk purchases, please contact Simon & Schuster Special Sales at 1-866-506-1949 or business@simonandschuster.com.

The Simon & Schuster Speakers Bureau can bring authors to your live event. For more information or to book an event, contact the Simon & Schuster Speakers Bureau at 1-866-248-3049 or visit our website at www.simonspeakers.com.

Interior design by Jill Putorti

Manufactured in the United States of America

10 9 8 7 6 5 4 3 2 1

The Library of Congress has cataloged the hardcover edition as follows:

Banks, David C.
  Soar : how boys learn, succeed, and develop character / by David C. Banks with G. F. Lichtenberg.
     pages cm
  1. Boys—Education. 2. Young men—Education. 3. Minorities—Education—United States. 4. Motivation in education. 5. Sex differences in education. I. Title.
  LC1390.B36 2014
  371.8211—dc 3   2014001813

ISBN 978-1-4767-6095-7
ISBN 978-1-4767-6096-4 (pbk)
ISBN 978-1-4767-6097-1 (ebook)

To all those who labor in the vineyard without ceasing, to ensure that our young men, our future, and our destiny are secured.

He was like an eagle hovering over its nest, over-shadowing its young, Then spreading its wings, lifting them into the air, teaching them to fly."

—DEUTERONOMY 32:11

CONTENTS

CHAPTER ONE

"SOMEBODY NEEDS TO HELP THE BOYS"

How Can We Stand Up for Young Men?

The knock came on the door of my elementary school classroom while I was sitting at my desk. Another student, one from my younger brother's class, brought in a note for my teacher. I knew what it said: "Could David please come speak to his brother? Philip is acting up again."

I had a good reputation in elementary school and I was considered mature for my age. Philip's teachers always seemed to think that if anyone could influence him, I could. And so I'd get up from my desk and follow the student monitor who had brought the note, out of the classroom and down the hall. The walk felt as if it took a long time. When my brother's teacher saw me, in front of the whole class she would say something like: "Your brother is not listening. He's not being respectful. I've spoken to him time and again! Soon I'm going to have to call your parents, but I thought I'd ask you first, David.

Maybe he'll listen to you." The whole speech was delivered in a tone that I knew drove Phil crazy. His classmates all stared.

My brother would get up from his seat, push in his chair, and the teacher would lead us out into the hallway, where she'd say more or less the same thing again. I would answer, "Yes, ma'am," and act as respectfully as I could. Phil wouldn't say a word.

Alone in the hallway, we'd both start talking really fast. I'd say something like, "What's the matter with you? Don't you know Daddy's going to come to school and get you? Don't you know he's going to whup your butt?"

He'd say something along the lines of "I didn't do it! It was so-and-so and he did this and I didn't do that, but she wouldn't listen. She's always blaming me! All I did was try to explain!"

We both talked at once, rapid fire, until Phil was called back inside. And so it went. Four times a year, we would get our report cards and bring them home. Mine would be full of 90s and 95s; his had several 55s and 60s. And this was head-to-head competition: my brother and I were only eleven months apart—I was born in January, and he was born in December—and we were in the same grade.

Our father was an involved parent, interested in what we had to say, and as an enthusiastic player in our recreational games, he was always ready to join us for football and such. But he was also a strict, old-school disciplinarian, most of all when it came to our grades. He himself had dropped out of high school and worked years at hard, low-paying, physical jobs, including stints as a shipping clerk and in a men's clothing warehouse. When they first married, my parents, like many young couples, couldn't afford their own apartment; they had to live with my grandfather. My dad came to see that dropping out of school had been an enormous mistake. In time, he earned a GED (a high-school equivalency degree) and started taking civil service exams, winning jobs in the post office, working as a conductor for the Metropolitan Transit Authority, and finally becoming a police officer.

That was considered a top-level civil service job, but he soon found that even in his success, he was limited in how far he could climb, how many promotions he could get. To overcome these limits, he studied part-time for many years, earning an undergraduate degree and taking some graduate courses.

Phil says that when he showed Dad his grades, there was no talking permitted. Phil might try to explain: "Dad, it's a lot of pressure, always going up against an honor-roll student like Dave," but our dad wouldn't hear it. Punishment was his response.

BOY ENERGY

Why wasn't my brother living up to his potential? I've had decades to think it over, as a brother, a father, a teacher, and a school principal. In part, I see now that he was the classic middle child, always in the first child's shadow. It was worse because we were so close in age. He would have been better off starting school the following September, but as it was, I was always among the oldest kids in my class, and he was always the youngest in his. I had that extra year of maturity going for me, and particularly for boys, maturity can take a while to kick in. Developmentally, he was a year behind in both academics and social maturity; we wondered when he would ever realize his potential. I had many chances to experience early success, while he rarely experienced even the small victories and moments of recognition that help motivate all of us to achieve greater things. He must have felt, from early on, *Why am I even trying to be an A student or a well-behaved kid? I'm never going to catch up to my older brother.* And so he tried to stand out as a smart-aleck.

Phil was not a terror, not out of control, not the kind of kid to get into violence, but he had a lot of energy, even more than the average boy. Part of that energy came from frustration. Energetic, often singled out by his teachers, frustrated—he could be a handful. The teachers tended to lose patience. As each in turn got to know him as an underachieving student and a provocative presence in her classroom, that became his identity. They looked for more of it. He heard an awful lot of "Stop it, Philip!"

As an adult, I found out from my parents that the teachers and the administration of our school had recommended that Philip be put on medication because, they said, he was "too hyper." They made the same recommendation for him that is made for lots of other active boys, black and brown boys most of all. Young men of color are three times more likely to be categorized as mentally retarded or learning disabled—black students, for example, represent 17 percent of students overall but 41 percent of those in "special ed" classes; and in those classes there are more than twice as many black males as black females.

This doesn't necessarily stem from racism or a bias against boys. The majority of teachers in this country are white and female, and their personal experiences give them little in common with boys like Philip. When they were girls, they probably liked school. Teachers approved of their behavior. They did well. For all those reasons, they may have been inspired to become teachers themselves, but the very strengths that qualified them to be teachers meant that they probably lacked the personal context for understanding a boy like Philip—either why he was so unhappy in the classroom or how his feelings could provoke him to behave in disruptive ways. The result, as Peg Tyre, author of *The Trouble with Boys*, described it, is that as early as preschool, "many young men get into a pattern of negative feedback . . . based on pretty normal behavior."

Anyone could see that Phil was actually very verbal, very quick-witted. In fact, his intelligence was part of what made him so hard for teachers—or anyone—to handle. When a teacher would give him a directive, he might tell her, "You're not my mother and you're not my father. You have no right to tell me what to do!" Just the thing to get under a teacher's skin—and to distract her from seeing the challenges he faced and the help he would require to reach his potential.

Philip was not just angry and mouthy in school, he was also bored. In my experience, smart girls who get bored often have the social skills to play along, but Philip, like a lot of boys, had trouble seeing the purpose in the distant end results of education. Many boys will ask themselves, *Why are we doing this? What's the point?* And when they don't find an answer, something practical they can see in front of them, instead of keeping their confusion and frustration to themselves, they act out. They are no less unhappy than the bored girls, but they are far more likely to get punished for it.

Had my brother been born to a different kind of mom and dad, he could have easily become a statistic. They might have given him medication to take away his energy, and then, once they'd slowed him down, the school could have put him in the slow class. That would certainly have made it easier for his teachers to teach, and it has happened to countless young men who never achieve the level of success that they should have. But my parents told the school administration, "Sorry, no. He's got a little extra energy but you're going to have to figure out how to deal with that."

Phil's grades were mixed, near failing sometimes, through middle school. In high school, he got them up into what could be called the average range, the sort of grades that make it hard to get into a good college. He was not a failure, but he was a chronically mediocre performer.

What could he do? Report cards came every quarter, at which point my father would be waiting at home to judge his grades. Philip had a close friend named Stephen who also struggled academically. Stephen was good at drawing, and he used to take his report card, which in those days was a paper card that the teacher filled out in pen, and touch it up a little before showing it to his mother. When it came to report-card forgery, some numbers were easier to work with than others. If Stephen received a 55, he could turn it into a convincing 85. If he got a 70, he could make it look like a 90. I don't think my brother forged his grades, but even today he talks about school as if there was no realistic solution, only the fantasy that he could fool all the adults. "If I had just found a way to con that school issue," he's told me, "life would have been fantastic."

I've asked him, "Couldn't you have found a way to get better grades?"

"That wasn't going to happen," he said.

For me, school couldn't have been much better. I was successful, well respected, and well liked. After I left elementary school, I kept in touch with my favorite teachers and my principal—and in fact, that school had only two principals in forty-five years, a remarkable measure of stability at a school that was in many ways excellent.

But to Philip and Stephen, it seemed hopeless, a rigged game. Their teachers couldn't help them, their parents couldn't help them, and the result over and over again was public humiliation and pain. Sometimes, my brother told me, he thought that the teachers and our father must enjoy having someone to punish.

And so, for years, the knock would come on my classroom door: another teacher asking me to "please do something about Philip." Even our youngest brother, Terry, who shared a bedroom with him, will tell you that when we were growing up, he wasn't sure how Phil would turn out.

I didn't like getting called to Phil's classroom. I was uncomfortable with that spotlight on me, on us both, as we tried and failed, over and over, to straighten him out. Nobody wants that kind of attention. I remember wondering, *Why are you making me do this? Why do you even put me in this position?*

I especially hated the way Phil, frustrated and embarrassed, would run his mouth. He would yell, "You're a *bastard*, Dave! Mom and Dad had you before they got married. So you're a *bastard!*" He would get under my skin until I just wanted to kick his butt.

One afternoon in the school yard he started in on that bastard stuff in front of everyone, and the next thing you know, I was beating him up. I punched him a couple of times and then held him down over a flight of concrete stairs. I could hear the excitement of the other kids watching—*Yeah, yeah! Beat him up! It's a fight!*

As I held Phil pinned with his head hanging over the first stair, I had him right where I wanted him. And then I thought, *This is my brother. I'm not supposed to be fighting my brother.* Sure, we would always have our little fights at home, but now I was fighting with him in public while other people, some of them strangers, yelled for me to do him harm. It was, maybe, the worst feeling I ever had in my life.

A SECOND CHANCE

As seniors, we both applied to college. I got into every school but one. Philip received rejection after rejection. Finally, on the way home from our school's senior trip, our dad told us, "Philip got accepted!"

"Yeah, Phil!" I said. "Wait, how do you know, Dad?"

"Some mail came in over the weekend, and I took the liberty of opening it!" My dad was super excited. I was excited for Phil, too. But Phil seemed only distantly pleased, as if this good fortune had happened to someone else.

Phil attended that school, Lincoln University in Oxford, Pennsylvania, which lays claim to being the oldest historically black college in the country. It was the school Chief Justice Thurgood Marshall attended, and also President Kwame Nkrumah of Ghana. Off in Pennsylvania, away from us, Phil transformed. He made the dean's list, became president of his fraternity, and established himself as a leader, a star on campus. He met his wife, Denise, and married her. He graduated a different man.

We both finished college and came home looking for our first jobs. I became a safety officer in a school. Philip drove a bus for the MTA, feeling very proud to have a job with benefits, before he took the test for the New York City Police Department and became a beat cop like my dad. I remember our grandma Pearl was so upset about the dangers of being out on the street. "You didn't go to college to walk around and be a cop!" she told him.

But my father encouraged Philip to see the police department as a career with long-term opportunities. In his own career, my dad always felt he lacked two things: a college degree and a mentor. But Philip had the degree and he had my dad, who was still "on the job," as they say in the police force, a lieutenant two ranks above Phil. My dad would tell him: white kids come on the job, and their dads or their relatives who came up ahead of them make sure they focus on studying so they can pass exams and win promotions, which mean more authority, more money, more influence, and the chance to do more for their families. He told Phil that too many young black officers don't have anyone higher up to mentor them, so they are just happy to carry a gun and wear a uniform, and to feel like a big shot in the neighborhood. They have no vision of their future.

Philip started taking the exams to qualify for promotion in the police department. He became a sergeant, and several years later a lieutenant. Now father and son held the same rank. Philip took the next test and was promoted to captain. That's when Dad retired—he said that when you have to salute your own son, it's time to go.

Soon, people who hadn't seen my brother in years started saying to me, "Philip? You've got to be kidding me! Philip was such a knucklehead! He's a captain now? He's an inspector?"

Philip had been a kid no teacher expected to excel at this level. But here he was the commanding officer of a police precinct. In New York City, there are a small number of what are called one-star chiefs, and even smaller numbers of two- and three-star chiefs. Above them all, there is one four-star chief, known as the "chief of department," who runs the day-to-day operations of the entire New York City Police Department and reports to the police commissioner, who is a civilian, a political appointee. In 2013, Chief Philip Banks became chief of department. This kid who seemed like he might miss his chance to go to college was now protecting the entire city of New York, and seeing his name on the short list as a candidate for police commissioner.

WHEN WILL THE LIGHT GO ON?

Watching Philip struggle for all of those years, then succeed when hardly anyone expected him to amount to much, taught me something I have carried with me ever since: never give up on a child. I was the sort of young man whose light went on very early; Philip was the sort whose light came on later. But in time, both shone brightly.

That experience of growing up with Philip has informed all my work in education, as a teacher, an administrator, and as the head of a foundation dedicated to improving education nationwide. It showed me that all of us have a responsibility to tend those flames, but that we must do so while never knowing when the fire is going to catch and that light is going to shine.

Are some of these boys going to tax us along the way? Sure. But later on, those very kids will be the ones doing remarkable things. Their teachers and their neighbors and others who knew them when may say, "Can you believe it?! Would you ever have believed it?!" But as someone who has run a school where young men do succeed, I say, yes, I believed it, even when they were at their most challenging. My work with those kids has confirmed that every child is a gift. Our job is to accept the responsibilities of that gift, to nurture those boys, to instill discipline, to love them, and to give them the tools to be successful. That's what we're supposed to be doing.

How will it play out? How can we know when the light will come on? We can't. We're never sure how it will go for this or that young man. We can't tell in the fourth grade or the fifth grade. We can't tell in the ninth grade or the tenth grade. What I do know is that among any group of young men, and especially among those in the most challenging environments, there are only a small number of Davids, who show their promise early on, and many, many more Philips, who make us wait. But each one offers us the chance to be part of a miracle, the miracle of a young man fulfilling his promise and his potential because he received the support and guidance that he needed.

WHO WILL STAND UP FOR YOUNG MEN?

This faith in the potential of young men, even those like Phil who struggled at first to soar, was what called me to work in education. That had never been my career goal. Back when Philip began building his career in the police department, I decided, after teaching for six years, to go to law school. After I graduated, I took a prestigious position in the New York Department of Law. I'd "made it," and now I had a family to support. But the call of education was ever present. So I kept my law job but I took night classes at three different graduate schools, earning my educational administration and supervision certificate in a single semester. I became an assistant principal, and in time the founding principal of the Bronx School for Law, Government and Justice, a new kind of partnership between the criminal justice community and an inner-city high school.

Bronx Law was part of a new generation of small, academically rigorous schools offering personalized instruction so our students wouldn't slip through cracks. As we grew from a first class of sixty-four boys and girls to a total student population of between four and five hundred, mostly from the South Bronx, I worked hard to establish my reputation as principal. I built a team of excellent teachers and staff, and nurtured a student culture in which the students helped one another to thrive. In time, I got the school running the way I wanted it to, and the city of New York provided us with our own building. It all came to feel very comfortable. I enjoyed it so much, I would have been happy to stay there as principal for many years.

What I hadn't expected at Bronx Law was that the applicants for that kind of academically rigorous school would be, overwhelmingly, girls. We looked up one day and realized that two out of every three of our students were female. Girls ran for most of the leadership positions, while the boys tended to sit back and let the girls be in charge. I was happy for the successes of the young women, but I was increasingly concerned for the young men, because what we were seeing at my school was part of an ominous national trend.

THE FEMINIZATION OF SCHOOL

Across this country young male students are struggling—and their parents and teachers often feel frustrated and helpless. In elementary and high school, American boys do less well on tests compared with girls, and the gap only grows as they get older. Boys have 70 to 80 percent of the behavioral problems. Boys are twice as likely to be left back and five times more likely to be expelled. The statistically average American college now has a female-to-male gender ratio of 60 to 40, and that gap too is growing. It's as if, in the American classroom, the girls have become the Davids, showing their promise early and following through to success, while the boys have become the Philips, seemingly destined not to live up to their potential.

The group of young men who experienced these trends first, and have been hit hardest, are young men of color. While the ratio of females to males attending American colleges has reached 60 to 40, at the traditionally black colleges it is now 70 to 30, and the gap continues to grow. Only 55 percent of black and Latino students graduate high school, and in most big cities, the rate for young men of color is well under 50 percent. In other words, for urban black and Latino men, *failure has become the norm.* And what happens to those who don't finish high school? Nationwide, almost two thirds of African-American males who don't graduate are unemployed—and more than half of those end up in prison.

Mass incarceration in this country has terrible costs both for those incarcerated and for the country as a whole. According to "Collateral Costs," a report by Bruce Western and Becky Pettit for the Pew Charitable Trusts, taxpayers are spending more than $50 billion a year on prisons, or $1 in every $15 from state general funds. Meanwhile, "incarceration eliminates more than half the earnings a white man would otherwise have made through age 48, and 41 and 44 percent of the earnings for Hispanic and black men, respectively." These men don't simply lose income during prison terms. They suffer a massive lifetime decline in income for themselves and their families. How do so many young men of color come to meet this fate? As I reported to New York City's former mayor Michael Bloomberg while serving as cochair of his Young Men's Initiative, a $127 million effort to illuminate the barriers faced citywide by young men of color, the gap is already visible in kindergarten. Falling behind at the start of the race can begin a dangerous cycle in which early setbacks provoke teachers and other authority figures to pull these students out of the mainstream, interrupting their efforts to succeed the way other young people do. Not only are they far more likely to be placed in "special ed," but black male students are more than twice as likely to receive a principal's suspension of one to five days out of school, and four times as likely to receive the more severe superintendent's suspension, which keeps them out of school for up to a year.

In all these ways, both black and Latino males find their journeys as students interrupted. From regular classes, they are moved to special education classes. Suspensions take them out of school and deplete their ability to succeed when they return. As these young men find themselves out of the game, and discover slowly and painfully how hard it will be to get back in, they rarely have words for what they've lost. They express themselves through frustration, by shutting down, or through violence. The resulting involvement with the juvenile corrections system may keep them out of school again, and for even longer stretches of time. If they are incarcerated as adults, that's just another in a series of diversions from the mainstream.

Often the adults whose work it is to help young people overcome obstacles only make matters worse. Parents who once struggled in school themselves may have lost faith that education can make a difference. Some oppose their children's education out of resentment, or out of fear that it will steal their children away. Teachers can be just as negative. I can't count the number of times I've been invited by a principal to speak at a struggling school, only to have the principal confide in me, *My teachers don't even believe in these kids.* Far too often, not just parents and teachers but school administrators, social workers, juvenile corrections officers, and other adults on whom these young men rely actually expect them to fail, or at least to remain mediocre. Out of a group of struggling males, these adults may select a few "good ones" whom they like personally and try to assist, but far too often the overall expectation is that inner-city males especially are just too hard to reach. And at worst, some believe that young men of color are "naturally" thugs, miscreants, and deviants—hopeless cases.

THE BOY CRISIS

But while this experience hits brown and black boys earliest and hardest, the underlying causes are increasingly shared by American boys of many backgrounds. Nationwide, the percentage of children growing up without a father in the house has tripled from 11 percent in 1960 to 33 percent today. Among African-American families, in 1920 that number was only 10 percent, comparable to that of other groups. In 1960, it was 20 percent, still significantly lower than the current figure for all American families. Today, it is 68 percent. Again, the trend started earlier for African-Americans, and hit harder, but that is the direction in which the entire country has been moving.

The discussion of young men in this country has recently reached a fever pitch, with books such as Kay Hymowitz's *Manning Up* questioning whether boys are even capable anymore of maturing into workers, husbands, and fathers worth having. Some journalists, like Hannah Rosin, have gone so far as to ask if we have reached *The End of Men.*

Years before that alarm was being sounded for men in general, I was aware that a large number of young men of color, including those in the South Bronx, where my school, Bronx Law, was located, were in serious trouble. Even as I savored the success of our girls, I felt a strong desire to help those boys.

For that reason, I joined the Legacy committee of the One Hundred Black Men, Inc., a civic organization of African-American professionals in New York City to which my father and I both belonged. Our goal was to found a public school that could do, for some of the young men who needed it most, what my brother needed as a child. It would be a chance to support the ones most easily misunderstood, the ones least likely to get their needs met, and to help them realize their potential in a typical school setting. It was through the efforts of the One Hundred Black Men that the first Eagle Academy for Young Men was founded, and I became its first principal.

Our inspiration came in part from a study that showed that 75 percent of the prison inmates for the entire state of New York were taken from the seven neighborhoods in New York City, including the South Bronx. To me that was an astounding statistic—even if 75 percent of inmates came from seven neighborhoods *statewide* I'd have been amazed, but the neighborhoods giving up so many of their young men to fill the state's prisons were all right here in the city where I'd grown up. In neighborhoods like those, young men often seem to be giving up on themselves. They learn to expect a life on the sidelines or worse.

Because it starts to feel inevitable, these young men learn not to talk about what is happening to them. The ones who do talk about it are their mothers. I have met mothers with stories like these at every Eagle Academy open house. They tell me, "My son was so sweet just a couple of years ago, so huggable. I could take him in my arms. And now he's growing and he's changing. I'm losing him to the pull of the streets. I'm losing him . . ."

What could we do for young men who might be going wrong? I'd read and heard so many eminent experts whose message boiled down to this: We can only wait. Wait until some far-off day when poverty is ended. Wait until the cycle of violence is somehow broken or the collapse of the family magically reversed. Other experts will tell you that we have to wait until we change the anti-intellectual culture of the inner city, the worship of thugs as heroes. Still others claim we have to wait until we can end the distractions that steal our children's time and attention, from drugs and alcohol to endless electronic devices. Or perhaps we have to wait until we solve masculinity itself, the difficulty of young men's impulsive, unmanageable energy. The list of problems—reasons to wait—is long indeed.

The One Hundred Black Men wanted to found a school that would prove those expectations wrong. We chose to concentrate our attention on the most underperforming group of young men—inner-city boys of color—so we decided to found Eagle Academy as a single-sex school in a "prison pipeline" neighborhood. We refused to cherry-pick the best available students, and we pledged to open our doors to all comers and let the New York City Department of Education decide at random who received a place in our school. Ultimately, 25 percent were classified as "special ed" for academic or social and emotional issues. Our mission was to show that, given the supports they need, young men can achieve excellence in both scholarship and character. They can graduate college-ready in overwhelming numbers. They can build productive lives. And so we had a double goal: to help young men in one of the most challenging neighborhoods, and to show, by helping them, that we could help any young man.

With the guidance of one of the first educational reform organizations in New York City, New Visions, which was funded in part by the Bill and Melinda Gates Foundation, and with the support of then senator Hillary Clinton, One Hundred Black Men prepared for our public presentations to make the case that the city should let us establish a school. Board member Buddy Johnson, a nationally acclaimed former school principal and school superintendant, remembers, "We held many meetings with parents and others in the community, many focus groups and discussion sessions. It's hard to recall how many meetings we held, all that time and effort to shape a school that would be high performing, with the community support to make it viable." There were no shortcuts.

During the time we spent making presentations to the city, out of all the different people who sat in judgment of the ideas we were offering I can hardly remember one man of color. I barely remember anyone on the other side of the table who had grown up in any of the communities where young men need our help most. That fact seemed partly to explain how the situation for those young men had become so bad, and it confirmed our commitment to making change by drawing on the strengths of those communities.

Each of us involved in creating Eagle found the areas where we could best contribute. Some got involved in shaping public policy on education by sharing our growing expertise and writing op-eds for newspapers. Some focused on the nuts and bolts of how a school runs: hiring the school leaders and the teachers, getting a space, formalizing a curriculum, establishing a budget. We had to keep pushing up our sleeves and putting in real time.

STRATEGIC PARTNERSHIPS

Before we ever tried to found Eagle Academy, others had made efforts to start all-boys public schools in New York. Those efforts failed. There was political resistance to the idea of doing something just for boys, who were assumed to be better off than girls. There were questions about whether it was even constitutional: Would a lawsuit shut down an all-boys school just as it was getting going?

It was clear we could not succeed without some powerful partners. And so, even as we learned to do as much as we could on our own, we looked for others who could help us. In New York City, control of public education had recently shifted from the Board of Education to the mayor. Mayor Bloomberg made it clear he wanted to make education a priority, and this became the basis for partnership: we both needed allies. The One Hundred Black Men offered the mayor our dedication to developing expertise on the education of young men of color. Our board president, Paul Williams, became part of the mayor's "kitchen cabinet" on education. That gave the mayor a chance to become more familiar with the ideas of our group.

In late 2003, the Legacy committee of the One Hundred decided to reach out to then senator Hillary Clinton. As soon as we made our presentation to her, it was clear she had a deep understanding of the value of what we were doing—she grasped the legal concerns about an all-boys school, but she was deeply impressed by the idea that the One Hundred Black Men were serious professionals standing up for the younger men in their home community. She pledged to be supportive in both big ways and small, and she talked about Eagle not just in New York and not just to audiences of color but all over the country, becoming our champion nationwide.

With Senator Clinton's support, we then met with Mayor Bloomberg. Now the mayor not only had some familiarity with the work of the One Hundred, he had the senator's personal recommendation that he take this project seriously. He met with us, discussed the issues, and in the end he said, essentially: "Let's go for it. We may get sued, but if so, we'll have the corporate counsel's office at the New York City Department of Law to defend it. This is worth fighting for."

I've mentioned some of Eagle's most prominent partners to suggest what is possible for a small, committed group with a strong, compelling mission, no matter where they begin. I would be remiss, though, if I didn't make clear that our most essential partners have always been the parents and other members of our school communities—some of whom partnered with us before Eagle Academy even existed. I remember when we were trying to launch the first school where I was principal, the Bronx School for Law, Government and Justice. A new schools chancellor had been appointed, and it looked as if our plans for the new school might be canceled. We rallied our community to come to a meeting at the chancellor's office, and the turnout was huge. We took up every seat except those reserved for the politicians. Tracy Lewis, a parent supporter, gave a memorable speech in which she said, "I am here today representing the future parents who don't have children in school yet." She described the difference that Eagle's success could make for the Bronx overall. At the end of the meeting, the school board president said, "In all my years, I have never seen a display like this. Truly impressive." All the members of the board shook our hands. The plans for Eagle were put back on the table, and after the school was finally established, Tracy Lewis ultimately became president of the Eagle Parent-Teacher Association.

THE EAGLE RECORD

After much effort, the One Hundred Black Men founded Eagle Academy in 2004. True to our original vision, it was a public school for boys, with no requirements for admission other than each family's expressed interest in having their young man attend. We have more than doubled the graduation rate for our population group. More than 90 percent of our graduates go on to college, and our success rates are improving over time. We have built on our success by opening new Eagle schools in Newark in 2012, Harlem in 2013, and Staten Island in 2014. Many of our graduates return to their schools and neighborhoods, to inspire and assist those coming up behind them.

BEYOND ISLANDS OF SUCCESS

Let me be clear: if the only story I had to tell was how one or even a few schools overcame the odds, I wouldn't have written a book. If I didn't believe that our experience could improve the lives of young men in varied communities—rural, urban, even abroad, where the most recent requests to partner with Eagle have come from—I wouldn't have written a book. I'm not all that interested in little islands of success. Stories of how individual teachers inspire their students and even stories of teachers who have inspired me are reflected in these pages, and I'm always impressed with excellent educators and deeply grateful for their work, but I've learned that a few exceptional educators are not enough. The sad truth, when you hear an amazing story about that one inspiring teacher in a failing school, is that most students were never in her class. A lone success—one exceptional principal, one inner-city kid who makes it big, or one family that beats the odds—may do great things, *but fundamentally, nothing changes.* The close-up on that successful face inspires us, but the bigger picture remains: the tiny number who find a way out and the vast majority who are essentially abandoned.

Many of us felt the painful urgency of this situation when we watched the documentary *Waiting for Superman,* which evoked the desperation of families hoping to get their children into a few elementary schools that offered the promise of a better future. That compelling film showed what was at stake and framed the question, What can we do? But the film only addressed elementary school students, not the long journey from elementary school through college and adult achievement. It didn't provide the answer.

Our answer begins with a change of mind-set. I remember attending the New York premiere of the movie *Malcolm X*, starring Denzel Washington. I was always highly inspired by the way Malcolm transformed himself from a street hustler who was only out for himself into a leader who saw the humanity in everyone. Malcolm once said, "Education is the passport to the future, for tomorrow belongs to those who prepare for it today," and that became one of the guiding principles for Eagle Academy.

When the movie ended and I came out of the theater, there were journalists conducting interviews. A South African reporter asked me, "Who do you think will be the next Malcolm X?" People ask this sort of question all the time. Who will be the next Martin Luther King, Jr.? Who will be the next Nelson Mandela or Barack Obama? Who's the next solitary hero in history's line? To me, that misses the whole point.

So when she asked me, I told her, "I am. I'm the next Malcolm X."

She looked surprised.

Then I pointed to my brother Phil, who was beside me. I said, "He's the next Malcolm X." I wanted the reporter to understand that there are many of us who possess the same drive, determination, and love for our communities that Malcolm had, and that the time has come to stop looking for the next one-in-a-million miracle. We need to think much bigger, and empower all the Malcolms among us.

To me, what matters most in my story is not founding Eagle Academy in the Bronx. That was just a step. After we made that school a success, we founded another Eagle school in Brooklyn, where Rashad Meade was the principal. A new group of different yet dedicated people took what we had learned and built on it and succeeded there. And then we founded a third Eagle school in Queens with yet another principal, Kenyatte Reid, and another committed staff, and they made it work again. In the Bronx, average attendance has been 90 percent; in the Brooklyn and Queens schools it's about 95 percent. We're getting better at this as we go along.

Again, I didn't write this book to trumpet the success of a few schools. I did so because of the knowledge we have gleaned as we have learned how to raise our students to soar—knowledge I can now share with all those who raise, educate, support, employ, and believe in young men, of any background, anywhere.

At Eagle, we certainly don't know everything. Our method is a constant process of new discovery of what our young men need and experimentation to find what will better help them to flourish. But fundamentally, as I will describe in this book, we have cracked the code. The Eagle method is not specific to race or socioeconomic status. It is a philosophy and a set of practical strategies that can be adapted to embrace and support young men of any background to achieve their promise and potential. It shows what we can all accomplish—in our homes and in our schools, in our community organizations and our businesses, in our towns and cities small and large—as we help shape the young people who will determine our nation's future.

That's no exaggeration. Where our young men are not succeeding, school ratings fall and take property values with them. Crime increases. Budgets strain to meet the cost of incarcerating our young people. Businesses struggle to find skilled workers, and retailers find fewer buyers for their goods. As education writers Richard Whitmire and Professor William Brozo have argued, "The marathon to produce the most educated work force—and therefore the most prosperous nation—really comes down to this: whichever nation solves the 'boy troubles' wins the race." Like it or not, the success of young men impacts us all.

If young men in this country sink under the weight of misunderstanding and wasted potential, our economy and our quality of life will sink with them. If our young men succeed as our young women have increasingly been able to do, then this country will succeed with them.

We don't need to wait on experts to conduct further studies. We don't need to throw up our hands in despair. I wrote this book to sound a call to action. If we can spread this message widely enough and act on what we now know, we can help restore our country's place in the global economy. Every young man can, and should, soar like an Eagle.

THE EAGLE METHOD

We start with this simple proposition: those young men who are struggling to succeed as scholars and as productive citizens, including young men of color raised in the most toxic environments and with fewer social supports, are like everyone else. They have the same wants, needs, and desires as other young people, the same joys and disappointments, and the same miraculous potential to flourish and to succeed in good-enough environments. They face exactly the same challenges as young people anywhere—plus additional challenges most others don't, a barrage of external environmental factors that, at their worst, can turn ordinary childhood toxic. What they need is the support to survive the toxicity of their local environments, so they can get back to the success for which they were intended.

This is less complicated than you may have been led to believe. Young men of color, and black males in particular, have been so overanalyzed in recent years it can sound at times like the "experts" think they have discovered a new species. But even many of the most challenging young men are not essentially different from other young people. They don't require special schools or some newfangled "experimental" curriculum. However, they do need to be taught in ways designed to reach those who are least prepared to get to college or to thrive there, and to be supported in making full use of their opportunities.

To do this, we have had to answer some very basic questions about young men:

- What do boys need if they are to blossom, both as scholars and as men?
- How can we make sure each young man receives the support necessary to overcome whatever threats his environment may pose, and to reinforce the gifts and strengths he already has?
- Where can families and schools find these additional resources to provide that extra reinforcement in a time of shrinking budgets and lowered expectations?

Who is this "we" I'm talking about? I want to be practical, and limit that "we" to those with a specific self-interest in how young men turn out—essentially, those with something to gain if our young men become productive leaders and citizens, and something to lose if they become a drain on our society. That means parents and teachers, school administrators and mentors, neighbors and employers, taxpayers and entrepreneurs, law enforcement officers and politicians, and anyone whose well-being depends on living on a safe street in a prosperous country. These are the people with an urgent, practical need to help turn our young men around, and that is a very large group indeed. We are all in the same boat. We will rise and fall together with our young men.

In this book I share many of the specific approaches we have developed to help young men succeed, from tapping into their natural competitiveness and peer sensitivity to providing rituals to help structure their days, from finding teachers who know firsthand the obstacles they face to expanding their sense of what the future might hold with guided travel and internship programs.

But if you read this book only to collect techniques for raising your own Eagles, you'll be left with a bigger problem: Who has the time? Who has the energy? And who can keep up the enthusiasm to do all of these things, consistently, for years? The fact is, most parents are already tired. Teachers work long days to fulfill their ordinary job requirements—how are they going to find it within themselves to do more? The peers that young men trust are often other misguided young men. Budgets are stretched, and our world is littered with increasing distractions for our children and ourselves, whether electronic, chemical, or whatever else. How can we do more for our young men when many of us feel we are stretched thin now?

The Eagle method, as I describe in this book, is to use every part to strengthen the whole. If it takes a village to raise a child, then our method is not just a guide to raising that child, but a system of mutual reinforcement for the hardworking villagers. After all, we are the ones who must show up, and keep showing up, if our children are going to get raised right.

As I describe in chapter six, it's not enough to get our boys a little mentoring. So many schools and organizations of all types use that word, and may even have what they call a mentoring program that may well be useful. But in our approach, mentors not only work to guide our young men, they do so in ways that support the teachers in the classrooms and the parents at home, that help our young men learn to keep themselves out of danger when they're away from school, and that make sure they seize opportunities to build an ambitious, practical future when those chances appear. Our mentors help to support everyone who is working to help our young men succeed—and as I'll explain, every part of the Eagle "family" pitches in to do the same. Every part strengthens the whole.

We begin to establish that larger system of support before we ever meet the young men whose families wish to apply. It begins when families hear the requirements for admission. In fact, there is only one requirement: a young man and a parent must show up at an open house and express interest.

We make those Eagle parents who meet this one requirement a promise. Will we take their son? Even if he struggles to read? Even if he's in "special ed"? Even if his old school promoted him just to get him out the door? Yes, we will take any young man because we can help any young man to succeed. That's our promise.

To some parents, it may sound at first like getting something for nothing. All you have to do is show up? But showing up is more demanding than it seems. We will keep asking them to show up as a family for the sake of their son's education, and in increasing ways. We need our students to join the brotherhood of Eagle students, as I describe in chapter three, and our parents to become true Eagle parents, committed to raising a scholar and helping to support our entire community of scholars, as I explain in chapter four. We need partners at home to support the work of our teachers and mentors. We need parents who will extend the reach and the strength of our school staff and administrators within the school, around the neighborhood, and out into the political landscape.

All that parents and potential students know at the start is that they must come to the school's open house in person, both parent and child, not just one or the other. In this way we begin to make clear that at Eagle we have our own way of doing things, and if you're going to become part of our family you're going to follow our rules—student and parent alike. By meeting that first requirement, families are making a kind of down payment on what will be a long, demanding, and essential commitment.

Do they understand all that? Not yet. Like you, perhaps, reading this book, prospective Eagle students and parents come to our open-house gatherings unsure about what they're getting into. But they do know that they wish for our young men and our schools to live up to their potential, and they want to discover how that can happen.

GOOD MEN

When I became principal of the first Eagle Academy in 2004, we didn't yet have our own school building. We had to share a building with the Bronx School for Law, Government and Justice, the school where I'd been principal until the year before and where the majority of students were female. Girls who had been my students would see me in the building and let me know, very clearly, how they felt now that I was no longer with them every morning at town hall meeting, visiting their classes, or reminding them of all they could accomplish. I had been like a father figure to those girls, and now many would call out to me, "You left us! You left us for those boys!"

My response was always "I didn't leave you. I'm going to straighten out the boys so you girls find some good men out there when you get older." Men who will be not just be good boyfriends but good husbands and fathers, good employees and entrepreneurs, good taxpayers and leaders and mentors to the next generation.

Often they came right back with "We don't want to hear it, Mr. Banks! You *left* us."

But girls who had graduated and then returned to visit tended to see it differently. They were out in the world, observing the state of young men. Studying and working alongside them. Dating them. When they came back to visit, they told me, "That's great, Mr. Banks. Thank God! Somebody needs to help the boys."

CHAPTER TWO

SAFE PASSAGE

Success in the Susceptible Years

For years, my parents, raising three sons, seemed to have what they needed for my brothers and me right there in the neighborhood. Then the well began to run dry, and they had to deepen their understanding of what kind of environment gives young men the best chance to achieve success—what puts them in danger and how to face those dangers when they appear.

I remember the day I felt something in my childhood world go wrong. I was eleven years old. It was afternoon and I was outside playing, as usual. Up until then, the Crown Heights section of Brooklyn—the world as I knew it—seemed to be everything a kid could wish. The games we would play! In the spring and summer we raced our bikes around the block and played marbles in the dirt backyards, and endless games of punchball and basketball. When it got cold we switched to football, two-hand touch. We played these games on the sidewalk and on the concrete of Sullivan Park, a courtyard shared by several tenement buildings. Behind our apartment building were the back alleys of Brooklyn, which connected all the backyards on our street to create another world for us in which to rip and run. That was where we played hide-and-seek, ringolevio, manhunt. All that for me was pure bliss—some of the best times of my life, just playing with my friends in the elementary school years.

That day it was late spring and the game was punchball—like kickball, except you punched the rubber ball and then tried to run around the bases. My team was in the field, and the hitter punched the ball so hard and high it flew all the way down the street to the corner. My friend Bernard took off after it. Runners were rounding the bases and my team was screaming for Bernard to hurry. But down at the corner, there were three older boys, strangers. One of them picked up our ball. Bernard ran up to him but the boy didn't give it back right away. He wanted to talk. We could see the four of them together down at the end of the block. By now, all the runners had scored.

Bernard was the kind of boy who ran everywhere he went, but that afternoon he walked the ball back to us.

"What happened?" we yelled. "What took you so long?"

"I just got drafted," he said.

"What do you mean?"

"I got drafted. Those guys are Jollystompers. They told me I had to meet them, and where to go and at what time tonight."

This was a generation before the Crips and the Bloods and the Latin Kings. The two big gangs rising at that time, the mid-1970s, were the Jollystompers and the Tomahawks. Bernard had just been recruited for a gang. I hadn't even known that could happen.

A few days later I was walking home from my middle school, Intermediate School 320, which was built on what had been the old Ebbets Field ballpark, where the Brooklyn Dodgers had played. My dad liked to tell me how he'd skip school and go to games when he was a kid—he saw Jackie Robinson, Roy Campanella, Sandy Koufax. "You know what it's like around Yankee Stadium on game days?" he would tell us. "The place is electric! That's what it was like right here. 1955—the Boys of Summer. Those guys all lived right in our neighborhood." I was always taken by that: Jackie Robinson lived right by my house.

As I continued on, I looked up and saw a stranger, a young man, sitting on the top step of one of the tenement stoops. He wore dark sunglasses and a big afro, and sat leaning back with his arms crossed and his feet up, watching us school kids file by like a king surveying his subjects. I'd never seen him before, but one of my friends beside me said, "Shh, go straight, go straight—don't even look. Don't you know who that is?" It was Sly, the leader of the Jollystompers. His name was enough to inspire fear, and now I had to walk right past him. I kept my head facing forward but I watched from the corner of my eye. He didn't smile. He looked straight ahead. *I hope he doesn't say anything to me. Don't let him say anything to me,* I thought as I kept walking. When I got to our apartment building, I didn't stay outside to play. I went right home.

Up till then I'd been like an eaglet, living safe in the nest, but on that day I lifted my head, looked around at the world, and saw there was danger. There were forces that could steal my childhood.

My parents were seeing changes, too. Store owners we had known my whole life were selling out and moving away. The great hamburger place down the block from school had closed. So had the deli that used to sell the bagels and lox, and the good corned beef and pastrami my father loved. There was no place for my mother to buy fresh fish anymore.

As stores closed, their buildings were no longer well maintained. Nor were the sidewalk and street in front of them. The feel of the entire neighborhood was changing. There had been a large Jewish community, including older people who liked to sit out on the sidewalk with their home attendants when the weather was pleasant, but now many kept indoors or moved away. Our great neighbors Al and

Phoebe, avid boxing fans who would take my brothers to the Golden Gloves tournaments, decided it was time to leave.

Then came a rash of burglaries in our own building, one apartment after another. The thefts started around the time that a new maintenance man began to work in the building, a big, tall guy. Not everyone made the connection, but my father was then a police officer on the beat in Ocean Hill–Brownsville, one of the most dangerous neighborhoods in New York. He recognized this man from the streets. My father said the first time he saw him, he knew this was a bad guy. Our apartment may have been spared, my father said, because the thief knew my dad was a police officer, so that if he broke in at the wrong time, he might be facing a gun.

My parents began to doubt that they could raise their three sons in Crown Heights. It was one of the most distressing feelings that parents can experience: that their ability to protect and guide their children was not enough, perhaps, to meet the challenges of their environment. But Crown Heights was by no means even one of the worst places in New York. My buddies and I worried about being tapped for gangs, but kids in Ocean Hill–Brownsville were getting shot. Plenty of parents in rougher neighborhoods were still dreaming of finding a way to bring their families to Crown Heights. For the time being, we stayed.

One day my mother gave me thirty dollars, what I thought was a lot of money, to buy my gym uniform, which was shorts and a T-shirt in the school colors. But the gym teacher was absent that day, so I kept the money in my pocket, planning to bring it back the next day. In the meantime, showing off to my friends, I flashed the cash. After dismissal, as I came out of school, an older teenager, much too old for middle school, came walking toward me and my buddies. I remember he had a bad left arm that he couldn't straighten all the way. It hung at an angle by his side.

He called out to us, "Come here, come here!"

My friends and I asked one another, "Who's he?"

Nobody knew, so we took off running across the street. But there were cars parked on the other side, so tight you had to jump up on the bumpers to get across. At least four of my friends made it over, but there were too many of us. In that bottleneck, this teenager with the bad arm caught me and two other guys. He pulled out a big knife and said, "If you move, I'll cut your throat."

The three of us stopped and he slowly looked over one of my friends. "You can go," he told him. Then he looked at my other friend and let him go, too. But he grabbed me and put the knife to my neck and he started patting my pants. He went right into my pocket and got my money. Someone who'd been at school that day must have told him, "See that kid right there? He has money in his pocket."

When I got home, I told my mother the money had been stolen. She didn't believe me. She was angry—I must have used it to buy something for myself, she said. She didn't think of our neighborhood as a place where children were targeted and robbed at knifepoint in the light of day. Once she and my father came to understand what had happened, they put that together with the other changes in the neighborhood. Unable to guarantee our safety, they finally lost the sense of security that a family depends on. *We could lose our boys to these streets*, they felt, as they started looking for a safer neighborhood.

My parents found us a new home in southeast Queens, on a tree-lined block of connected Tudor-style houses. But as you might expect, my brothers and I didn't want to leave Brooklyn. Our world was our friends on Montgomery Street, and we couldn't imagine giving them up. To this day I remember how it felt on that hot summer day we went to say goodbye. Our friends were playing softball in Sullivan Park, and I stood outside the fence, looking in. I called out to them, trying to explain that my brothers and I were going to camp for two weeks, like we had the summer before, but we weren't coming back.

My friends called over their shoulders, "See you later!" They barely looked up from their game. They didn't seem to understand what a big deal this was. My father told me, "You'll make new friends," trying to reassure me, but at the time I wondered how he could say that. My buddies and our games were my whole world.

In time, though, I found that my father was right. I did make new friends. It wasn't hard—my parents had found us a new block full of families with kids around the same age, and they were much like the kids back in Crown Heights. They played most of the same sports and games we had played in Brooklyn. Many of their fathers were civil servants, like mine—firefighters, letter carriers, police officers. Their parents were mainly still married, and though they'd brought their families from different parts of New York, they shared the same dream: to make a better life for their teenage kids.

I do remember that when we first got to Queens, I was confused by the narrow sidewalks—how could a group of kids walk side by side? I wondered. Were we allowed to walk in the street? I had to ask my father. He said sure, walk in the street. That was okay here. And soon it all felt like home, mostly because we fit right in.

So many kids! My mother used to say that in Queens you could drive twenty blocks in a row and each block would have a few kids living there, but then you would reach one block where it seemed as if the whole neighborhood lived. That was our block, with its attached houses. We had over fifty kids who lived right there, so when school was out there were always plenty of kids playing and hanging out. The rest of the neighborhood learned that this was the place to come when you were looking for a game, and that attracted everyone to 223rd Street. Soon we thought it was the best block in the world.

SUCCESS THAT FEEDS ON ITSELF

Though the kids on that block went to several different schools in and outside the neighborhood, we grew into a remarkably tight-knit group, looking out for each other and competing with each other. It seemed everyone was looking to do well. We competed in basketball and bowling leagues, in run-catch-kiss with the girls, and later, in dating. Some of the kids who went to the local high school did well academically because other kids on the block were doing well and they didn't want to be outdone.

It wasn't a utopia. Knuckle sandwiches were served at times. We learned how to fight, learned how to date, learned how to keep our grades up, and we learned it was our responsibility to help raise each other. As a teenager, I had a longtime girlfriend on the block who dreamed of becoming a doctor. I planned to be a lawyer. And growing up on that working-class block in Queens, under the watchful, demanding eye of that community, that's just what we did. Many young people thrived. Not all of us became heart surgeons, of course, but we didn't wind up in jail or strung out on drugs. We became productive citizens, as our parents hoped.

"Are you going to graduate?" wasn't even a question on our block; it was a given. One of my neighbors was a below-average student, but he was our buddy and we encouraged him when he was struggling. He never got left back. Without that constant support on the block, I can't imagine that he would have gone to college. He would have barely graduated high school. It took him seven years to finish college but he made it and now he's a corrections officer at Rikers Island. He owns his own home, pays taxes, supports a family, and he's doing well. I credit a lot of that to our block. On 223rd Street, the odds of us making it increased exponentially. As my father liked to say, there are no guarantees, but parents owe it to their kids to increase the odds by putting them in the best environment they can.

SIMILAR BOYS, DIFFERENT OUTCOMES

Back in the old neighborhood, although the kids shared similar experiences, things turned out differently. The worst example was two brothers who had been buddies of ours, Robert and Winston. They were both chunky boys, with short cropped haircuts and round faces. Robert especially used to hang out with us, and after we left, friends back in Crown Heights would give us news of him from time to time. We heard that Robert was using drugs. Then we heard he was dealing. When we were in our early twenties, Phil heard through his police contacts that Robert had been murdered. He wasn't just shot or stabbed. He was beheaded. The story was that he had been involved in a drug deal that went bad, and he owed a major Columbian drug dealer money. So the dealer made an example of him.

Stephen, our old friend from Crown Heights, was now manager of a movie theater. After Robert was killed, Stephen would let Robert's brother Winston into the theater for free. Stephen could tell something wasn't right with Winston. Not only had he lost his brother, but he was using drugs himself. Eventually, he wound up in a mental institution. From what I've heard, he will probably never get out. Both brothers were lost.

It's a terrible story, the kind of thing it's hard to believe about someone you used to play with after school. But in one way, the story wasn't a surprise. Robert was our friend, and we all remembered what he was like—always looking for an advantage, always trying to "get over on you," as we called it. He wasn't a bad kid, but was always looking to cut corners.

I remember playing marbles with Robert. The game of marbles was a big deal for us. We would go out into the back alleys behind our apartment buildings and draw a big circle in the dirt. Everyone brought their own collection of marbles, and you had to shoot one of yours into the circle with your fingers and try to bounce someone else's out of the circle while your marble stayed in. If you were successful, you won the other player's marble. You could take it home. The game required a lot of skill and practice, learning the best angles to shoot from, and learning to flick your finger with a certain touch. All the guys would sit around and watch the game.

The marbles came in all different colors and blends of colors as well, but they were the same size and shape. That was what kept the game fair. One day Robert showed up with a set of silver-colored marbles. We had seen silver marbles before, but although these, sold under the brand name Zion, were the right size, they were denser, heavier. Zion marbles could pop the other marbles out of the circle much more easily. It was like in basketball, when one team would bring in a player the other team didn't know, and it would turn out he was a much older, more experienced player, someone who really shouldn't have been playing with us lightweights. We called those guys ringers. Robert had brought in ringer marbles, but we didn't know it. We all kept playing. Robert kept winning. By the end of the day he'd won it all, every single marble. He walked home with his pants pockets bulging.

When I heard that Robert had run afoul of a major drug dealer, it made a sad kind of sense. That same habit of trying to "get over" on people that Robert had as a boy, he still had as a man. No one had taught him to conduct himself any differently. Had he remained that way but moved somewhere else, a neighborhood without hard drugs and weapons, he might only have gotten himself into a fistfight now and then. But having that nature, unchecked and unguided and in a neighborhood where the stakes were very high, it was probably just a matter of time before he tried to "get over" on someone in a situation where the consequences could be devastating.

NEGATIVE PEER PRESSURE

Teenage boys feel a deep need to gain the respect of their peers. More than at any other age, they adapt themselves to the culture around them. My brothers Phil and Terry and I talk sometimes about what it would have been like if we had still lived in Crown Heights, hanging out with our old friends, when they were getting into drugs and crime. Philip has said, "If Robert got into carrying guns when Stephen was still there,

Stephen could have gotten caught up in it. And if Stephen got into carrying guns, I would have gotten caught up in it, too." It's not that hard to
imagine. There is no one more susceptible to the influence of his friends
than a teenage boy. The odds for our safety and our success would have
been very different. Moving to that block in Queens may have saved our
lives.

It's not just a matter of a young man's physical safety. Growing up
with negative influences like the ones I described takes a toll on the
parents, who feel embattled about their children's safety as well. When
parents worry that their children may leave high school and get into
serious danger, they often come to feel that if they relax their vigilance
and discipline at all, if they let up even a little bit on their kids, they
could lose them. The mind-set becomes: *In this place, if I lose him, I
can't get my boy back. He's gone forever.* But while my father was in some
ways a traditional disciplinarian, when I remember him in Queens I
remember him and the other fathers moving their cars so kids could
play football in the street, and sometimes joining us for a little while
as guest quarterback. There was a feeling that all the parents could
ease up a little and enjoy the life going on around them. That ease
also made it possible for them to take the approach to discipline that I
describe in chapter seven, one that emphasizes teaching and guidance,
not strict control.

It might seem so far as if I'm telling a simple story, a fairy tale
with an easy lesson: if the world's neighborhoods are divided into
good and bad, the first step for raising young men is to make sure
you raise them in the good ones. But the truth isn't so simple. Our
new block, 223rd Street, was no paradise. My father was a beat cop
with three children, and my mother was a secretary—we were fortunate that they had the means to take us out of Crown Heights
and buy us a house, but those means were modest. Our new block
was safer, but the park a few blocks away looked like trouble to my
policeman-dad's eye, and he encouraged us not to play there until

we got a little older. Gangs were active in the area, though not right on our block as they had been in Brooklyn. When 223rd Street had a block party and people came from all over, I would recognize some of the really tough guys. Even then I knew: it only takes one spark to set off an explosion. You just had to pray that everyone would be well behaved, that even the bad guys would be good guys for the night of the block party.

Beyond the drugs in the neighborhood, the public schools nearby were weak academically—my father had to ask his contacts in the Board of Education to arrange for us to ride a bus for fifty minutes every morning to go to a better school. In winter, we had to be up and out of the house when it was still completely dark outside. Even with that special accommodation, my mother always said she wished they could have afforded to send us to private school.

Philip and I agree that the move to Queens probably saved our lives, but don't try to tell that to our youngest brother, Terry. Back then, he felt that leaving Brooklyn was pointless. He loved our life in Crown Heights, he was happy with his friends and games, and he felt safe. He was the baby eaglet with his head still down in the nest, thinking everything in the outside world was just fine. To him, when my mother and father picked us up at summer camp and brought us not to our home on Montgomery Street but to some strange new place in another borough of New York, it was a slick trick to get us to where *they* wanted to be—a house rather than an apartment. He still remembers how my father had to drive us all back to Brooklyn the first few weekends in a row, because we were so torn up about leaving. I think Terry was hoping each time that our parents would come to their senses and go back home to Crown Heights, where his life had seemed perfect.

Terry's not the only one who speaks highly of the neighborhood we fled. While working on this book, I went back to Montgomery Street, to see what memories it would conjure. Right in front of our old apartment building, I ran into someone from the block, Wayne, who was a few years older than me. Wayne had lived almost his entire life in Crown Heights, and he was grateful for it. "This particular block," he told me, "this particular neighborhood raised us up for not going to jail, not being a dope addict, not being strung out on drugs. I've been in Bed-Stuy, East New York, and all those neighborhoods, and thank God my mother got us out of there."

Wayne still remembers the horse-drawn fruit carts that came down the street when he was young, and how, if one of the kids attempted a little harmless theft and stole an apple off the cart as it went by, a neighbor would usually be there to grab that kid and set him straight. Wayne said that the community on our block taught him he couldn't do wrong and get away with it. He told me, "You know how it takes a village to raise a child? This was my village. This block saved my life."

I was surprised to hear him talk that way about the neighborhood from which my family had fled, just as I was surprised when I realized that our little brother, Terry, didn't see the point of our moving away until much later. Was our old block a good neighborhood or a bad one?

I sat down with my brother Philip to try to sort it out. Were we wrong? As we talked it over, we realized that Wayne was about seven years older than we were. When Phil and I were twelve and thirteen, and things were getting rough on Montgomery Street, Wayne was going on twenty. He was grown. And what we have both seen—Phil in his police work and me in the schools I've run—is that young men are most vulnerable to a dangerous environment for a short time, roughly the teenage years. That's when the peer pressure can be overwhelming. That's when they have an almost irresistible impulse to roam and explore and test out their growing bodies and minds to discover what they are capable of. That's when they are most likely to do something impulsive and unwise that could change the course of their entire lives.

As Rashad Meade, founding principal of the second Eagle Academy in Brooklyn, likes to say, "Thirteen is the age when young men start making some tough decisions." They venture farther and get exposed to a wider range of influences than younger boys. They are old enough to take on some responsibility, which can be for good or bad. A mother might start sending her son out to do errands she wouldn't have suggested before. A drug dealer might see the same potential—to deliver a package or to keep a lookout. That's why the Jollystompers recruited my friend Bernard during a punchball game. That's why their leader, Sly, was surveying my classmates and me as we walked home from middle school. We were on the verge of becoming useful. And at that age, young men's own motivations are starting to change as well. Thirteen isn't grown, but it's grown enough to get seduced by a pair of sneakers. It's grown enough to decide you're willing to do something you've never done before in order to get them.

At the time my family left Brooklyn, Wayne was already on the far side of that divide—just old enough that changes in the neighborhood weren't an immediate threat to him. He had "aged out" of the dangers of gang life, among other threats. In a similar way, my little brother, Terry, was safe on the younger side. Even in the roughest neighborhoods, if a boy has a parent close by to keep him out of physical danger and to explain the frightening things he may sometimes see, the child is likely to be all right. The danger zone comes when a young man's life starts to revolve less around his family and more around his peers, who may know as little as he does about the risks he faces, and feel just as impulsive.

SAFE PASSAGE

Behind the fairy tale of the "good neighborhood," the reality is more like this: every community poses some risk. There are alcohol and drugs and criminal temptations in wealthy neighborhoods as well as in poor ones; in urban, suburban, and rural areas. It's striking to me, when I visit some of this country's most sought-after colleges and universities, the ones we dream of our students attending, that their administrators must work constantly to help students avoid the dangers of hazing, alcohol and drug abuse, rape, suicide, and other threats. The question for young men about a neighborhood or a school is not simply whether it is "good" or "bad," but whether they can be helped to find safe passage through it. And the question for parents and educators is whether they can identify those threats and guide their young men through.

For my parents, Crown Heights became a place we had to leave not because it posed dangers, but because those dangers were more than they were able to help my brothers and me face and to overcome. That experience was something we shared with many of our new neighbors on 223rd Street. I remember our neighbor Janice, also by chance from Crown Heights, who became a close friend of our family. By the time they moved to Queens, her parents had become so frightened by the activity around them that Janice wasn't allowed off the family porch, night or day, unless it was to go to a supervised activity such as a Girl Scouts meeting or an ice-skating lesson. That meant she spent a lot of time on that porch, overlooking her mother's rose garden. Since she was out there anyway, her mother asked her to keep an eye on the people walking by, who sometimes picked her roses. Janice would sit on the porch, and when passersby got too close to the flowers, she would call out, "What? *What?* I never promised you a rose garden!" It's a funny story about a very serious situation, in which parents felt they had to keep their child almost housebound to keep her safe.

Even after our families moved to Queens, dangers remained and the rules for avoiding them were similar, but now the "porch" was bigger. It encompassed our whole block. My father put up a hoop and we played basketball in the common space behind our homes. One of the

neighbors, a man who worked nights, complained that the bouncing
ball and the shouting kept him awake when he needed to sleep during the day. But my father told him, "They aren't going to that park.
They're going to stay right here where we can see them." After that,
we played all our sports and games up and down that block, where
the gangs didn't come, and where a parent could always look out the
window and check on us.

Unlike today, there were far fewer video games. Kids were always
looking to play outside. The rule was that you had to have your
homework done first, and on weekends and vacations you couldn't go
outside before eleven in the morning. Then we'd head out and play all
day, almost every sport you can imagine. I remember my mother sent
us to take tennis lessons at the local high school, though I thought it
was a game for white kids. Once we learned, we kids even chalked a
tennis court on the street and played without a net. In time, I won
some tournaments.

Other times we made go-karts. We'd get up on Saturday and look
for old busted shopping carts so we could use the wheels. Then we'd
make up our carts with old pieces of wood. There was one father on
the block who had a garage full of tools and the things you would
want to build a kart. Mr. Jones would watch you, see you were doing
it wrong, and let you do it that way until you saw it wasn't going to
work. Then if you asked him to help, he'd pitch in. Once we made the
go-karts, we raced them.

In different ways, all the parents on the block encouraged us to
play outside, but nearby, with an adult eye on us. If we were playing
football, a father coming home from work might take off his jacket
and sub in for ten minutes. My friends today still talk about Mr. El-
lison, Mr. Stewart, Mr. Payne, and that whole crew of father figures
who would come out on the block and throw the football with us.
"Here comes Mr. Stewart!" "Yo, we got Mr. Banks!" They wanted us
to enjoy ourselves but they also knew that if we were on the block

and occupied with something we enjoyed, we weren't somewhere else, at risk.

At one point my father had tried to start a limousine business, but he couldn't find enough clients, so he used the car to take the whole block bowling and roller skating. One kid on our block became a high school football star, and his father would take five or six guys from our block who didn't go to his school to the games to root for Anthony. These were ways to give us activities we liked, where we almost didn't notice that we had an adult chaperone. Yet again, we were kept in safer situations and prevented from having a lot of empty, unsupervised time. My dad liked to say, "Idle time is the devil's workshop." But if you had asked me and my brothers at the time, we would have said it was a cool day. We saw Anthony lead his team to victory! We went roller skating! We weren't thinking about safe passage, but we had it.

A MENTAL MAP

In almost any neighborhood, the challenge is the same: some areas are safe enough for young men, but others pose serious risks of some kind. Parents need to draw themselves a mental map of the areas that are safest for their young men. To make that map, start with your home and work outward. Which neighbors' homes are safe? Which routes to and from home are safer? What are the safest outdoor spaces for sports and other play? What local activities and programs are well supervised? Then sit down with a calendar and think your way through a typical week. What are the paths your young man will take? When during the week are your sons likely to wander outside of the safest areas?

As boys grow, and they range farther and develop new interests, and as the seasons and the years change, that map of safer passages will start to feel too limited. It will be necessary for parents and sons alike to keep researching new possibilities—to talk to your friends, neighbors, extended family, teachers, coaches, camp counselors, librarians, the staff at the community centers, the offices of local politicians, and anyone else who knows your neighborhood, and ask all of them: Where can a young man my son's age spend some time and enjoy himself safely? What's the best way to get there and back again? How can he avoid the dangers he may encounter?

Look for opportunities to team up with other families trying to answer the same questions—maybe you could help form a building association or a block association, and gather with other parents to compare notes about providing safe passage for your children. Or start smaller: if there are dangerous hours when your son can't be at school or at home, maybe you could partner with another family and take turns supervising your boys. Maybe each of four families could take the children for one Saturday afternoon a month, so all your sons can experience what each family likes to do, whether it's a ball game or a trip to a museum.

Get the young man involved in the research, too. What would he like to do? Where could he do it? What do his friends know about doing it? If he has a passion for basketball, chess, or drawing, he should be out there helping to find out where kids like him go to do the things they enjoy. Given activities that appeal to them, young men are more likely not only to keep out of danger, but to feel that they have worthwhile lives they want to protect by heeding their parents' rules.

The goal is not just to set clear limits or to redirect young people from more dangerous activities to less dangerous ones. The goal is to model a satisfying, healthy lifestyle as part of a community. One of the first things my father did when we moved to Queens was to start a block association. He had a vision of the entire block as an extended family, and in response the members made him the association's president. The block association organized block parties with activities and prizes for every age, visits from the Jazzmobile (a mobile jazz concert under the stars), break dance competitions, and rap music performances. Those experiences were valuable for the young people on the block not just because we had some great evenings with great cultural events, but because they showed us how we could spend our time. Following the adults' lead, some of us kids started our own junior block association. We divided ourselves in two groups (Phil and I were always on opposite teams) and organized competitions, from a basketball league to a bowling league. We had a club we called the Silly Club, a kids' organization with officers, rules, and dues, where we played music and danced.

When I look back on those years on 223rd Street, the most remarkable thing might be how much time the teenagers on that block spent together. Sometimes on weekends we would sit out under the trees at night, talking until midnight, looking at the stars. We would just talk and joke around, "snapping on" each other—teasing each other, like siblings in the best way. That was where we wanted to be, in that group with young people we enjoyed and cared about, protected in that safe space. After years of our parents showing us the way, we had learned—even as teenagers!—that we could enjoy, in fact cherish, a responsible life within a safe and loving community. I think this was probably the best guarantee of our safety in the teenage years that anyone could have given us.

MAKE YOUR HOME A DESTINATION

Our parents made a special effort to turn our home, the safest place we knew, into a destination that we and our friends and extended family would want to visit. My parents picked our new neighborhood in part because there they could afford a house big enough that they could bring others in, rather than sending us elsewhere. Because of his police work, my father was always aware of the potential risks in other people's homes—not just lack of supervision but child abuse and pedophilia. Once they bought our house, they got a pool table, a Ping-Pong table, and whatever else they could afford over the years to make our home appealing to young people, so my brothers and I didn't want to spend the night elsewhere. If we wanted sleepovers, we had to have them at our place. We were always having friends and cousins stay over, and everyone was encouraged to join the conversation, adults and kids all talking at once. (Sometimes we had to explain to a shy visitor, "If you want to talk, just jump in!")

My cousins would say we were lucky we had such a happy household, but it was by my mother's and father's design, and it took constant effort. My mother was home with us a great deal of the time. They both sacrificed a lot of their own socializing, a lot of cocktails and card games and evenings out, for our benefit. If they'd let us socialize more at other kids' homes, my parents could have had a lot more "date nights." But they were focused on providing safe passage, day and night.

It would be a long time before I understood all the layered commitments my parents made—to their children; to their marriage; to making their home a place where other children would come to play, so my parents could supervise; to a level of expectations and discipline that required consistent attention and creativity; to their neighbors' families; to their block association; to their relationships with the police officers who patroled our block.

The challenge for them was to combine rules about where we couldn't go with ways to make us enjoy staying close to home. It wouldn't have worked if they had only forbidden us to leave. They had to inspire us to stay.

SAFE PASSAGE: A GUIDE

How can we provide safe passage for our young men, not just during the school day but around the clock and throughout the teenage years? That had been my parents' question when they left Crown

Heights, and when we founded Eagle Academy we had to ask it again, not just for a family but for an entire school.

We knew that no parent, teacher, or administrator could anticipate every place that teenagers could get to and all of the possible risks they might find there. And there was no question of moving our students to a "good neighborhood"—the vision of the One Hundred Black Men organization was to build a successful school in a rough neighborhood, the type where it can seem almost as if some young men were put on earth to fill prisons. That meant building a school in an environment where good kids, talented kids, kids with great teachers and dedicated, involved parents, were at risk of making life-changing mistakes every day.

So we approached safe passage from the other direction. One of the main reasons that kids in "better neighborhoods" get into less-serious trouble less often has nothing to do with the kids or the parents. It's that they aren't exposed to trouble as often. The environment simply isn't as risky. So although those young men are still teenagers, and still likely to make some naive and impulsive choices—let me say it: some dumb choices—those kids are usually pretty well out of harm's way. But in the neighborhoods around Eagle schools, there is serious risk. Lives can be shunted down a damaging path in one afternoon, one mistaken evening. Tragedy doesn't even require bad intentions. A student could be asked along on an outing, the point of which is unknown to him. Or he might choose to go knowingly because on television and in hip-hop videos, a drug deal or a break-in or other crime looks exciting and cool. Maybe he's just curious. Maybe he's scared to say no. Maybe he's bored and lonely and he'd rather not be walking the streets by himself.

So he goes along for some reason or for no reason and then things go wrong—a fight starts, a weapon goes off, and the police appear. And now this kid who was curious or bored or lonely, who thought maybe he'd have a little excitement, instead has a criminal record, or worse. An hour spent in the wrong place, and a life has been changed.

To prevent those kinds of tragedies, we took an approach that for me went back to the example of the parents on 223rd Street. We worked to give our young men a place that was worthwhile for them and at the same time physically safe—and then to keep them there as much as we possibly could. This is not altogether different from what my friend Janice's parents were doing when they told her, back in her Crown Heights days, that if she wasn't at a supervised activity she had to be in the house or on the family porch by the rose bushes. It's not all that different from what my cousins and uncles would do growing up, staying late at the community center to play sports or make art whenever they could, making it their personal oasis. But in adapting it to a school setting, we had two specific goals in mind.

First, to cover the entire day. Unlike a typical school that lets students out at two or three in the afternoon, Eagle's hours of operation go all day. Though the exact hours vary a bit among our schools and based on the age of the students, Eagles are generally with us from 8:00 a.m. to 5:00 p.m., plus many Saturday mornings.

Extending school hours is popular now among educators as a way to get students more study time, out of recognition that even some of the best students in America are finding it hard to compete globally because they are spending less time reading and writing and studying than students elsewhere. In the same way, lots of organizations now sponsor afternoon activities for youth. Some are doing great things. But while I see the benefits of giving young men extra class time and study time, and also stimulating after-school experiences for a day or two a week, we start with a more basic goal: to reduce the chance that serious trouble will find our young men by keeping them occupied and with us all day long. If they're in the school building, they are off the street. And that can make all the difference.

Even the timing of dismissal from school is designed to promote safe passage. If our students were let out when other schools let out, they would be on the street with an enormous wave of young men, some of whom live in ways that directly contradict what we're teaching—a kind of anti–role model. That's not what we want our students to see at the end of the day.

Our young men are dismissed at the end of the work day, and they share the streets and the buses and subways with a work crowd as opposed to a school crowd. They have plenty of working adults traveling with them.

If students leave us at five or six, then by the time they get home, they are hungry for dinner and they will go inside. After dinner, they are going to feel tired from their long day at Eagle, and that is by design. We wear them out, not just with classes and tutoring and study sessions but with after-school sports and other exciting, high-energy activities. Our long, tiring days in a safe place help keep them off the streets at night, too. They're safe in bed and soon it's morning, and they come back to us again. That's a model for safe passage through a full twenty-four-hour day. That's the kind of planning any parent of teenage boys might want to consider.

Other young men in different neighborhoods might not face such explicit physical dangers, but rather unsupervised access to drugs, alcohol, and automobiles, or other kinds of trouble. We make it our responsibility to know what our boys are up against, and to create a schedule to give them the best chance of coming through safely, every day. We try never to forget that each time we have to send them out onto the streets early, there may be consequences. As Principal Meade puts it, "Every day we have to do an early dismissal, I keep my fingers crossed."

GET BACK TO SAFE GROUND

Of course, no matter how hard we work to keep our students in safe places, there will be days when they leave those safe areas and no staff member or family member is there to look after them. We have to arm them with the understanding that will help them avoid and resist the dangers they will inevitably face. Before our young men start their first academic year, they attend a summer orientation we call Summer Bridge. At the start of that program, teachers lead a "field trip" through the neighborhood, pointing out the safest route to walk. We don't assume that they know, even if they grew up a few blocks away. We not only show them the way but also explain how and why we have chosen it.

We must also show the boys that even when they get into dangerous circumstances, they still have some choice in how they respond to them. We share stories of our own experiences with the students. I like to describe the time I walked past Sly, the leader of Jollystompers, back when I was a kid. That day, there was nothing I could do to keep him off my block or to stop him from taking an interest in me and my classmates. But I could choose to keep my focus, to resist my impulse to stare at him and attract his attention. I could keep walking. That's an important lesson for young men anywhere: they will encounter real dangers. It's up to them to keep their eyes open, to make it their business to recognize when there is danger nearby, to choose not to engage it. We tell them to get themselves back to safe ground. We also bring law enforcement agents into the school to share strategies for avoiding involvement with gangs, and how to conduct oneself, both physically and verbally, when stopped by the police. We provide complementary resources for parents on these same topics, all tailored to the specific situations we know our young men may encounter. Many of our teachers, as well as the professionals who participate in our mentoring program, grew up with similar dangers. They can talk credibly about the choices a young man makes when he's neither at home nor at school. Sometimes small bits of local knowledge collected from adults who grew up where our young men are growing up can make a big difference. In New York City, for example, gang members generally ride in the last cars of a subway train. We tell our students, "If you have to take the subway home, ride in the middle cars."

The key is to keep providing informed adult perspectives, so our young men can prepare for an encounter before it happens. Any adult can contact the local police precinct and ask if they will send an officer to a school or other organization to talk about preventing crime and managing encounters with the police. There are organizations for officers of color, who will often volunteer their time to talk to a group that has special interest in their perspective. The heart of their message is likely to be this: take some time to imagine what is going through the minds of police officers when they stop a possible suspect. The police tend to be younger adults who have their own families for whom they feel responsible. Their family's biggest worry for them on the job is for their own safety. The officers don't want to get hurt because they weren't cautious enough. If they stop you, they won't know right away if you're a bad guy or a good guy. So what you need to do if you are stopped is to work to avoid a situation where an officer may think someone is going to surprise them with a deadly weapon. Your goal when dealing with the police is to reassure them that you are not a threat.

At the workshops we hold at Eagle, we do role-playing exercises. *Pretend you are in a car with your friends. A siren goes off, and you pull over.* Or, *A knock comes on your door. It's an officer in uniform . . .* When you are confronted by the police, you may feel angry. You may feel threatened. You may want to yell, "What are you stopping me for? I didn't do anything wrong!" But your loud voice and your anger will only heighten the officer's fear that things could get out of control. Instead, be polite. "Yes sir, Officer." Keep your hands visible so it's clear you're not trying to pull out a weapon. Don't get out of the car until instructed. Make no sudden movements. Help them to see that you are not the threat they fear. If you follow these instructions, it can save your life.

*   *   *

Some of what keeps our young men safe are the physical signs that they are already on a path, already committed to a larger group. Rudy Coombs, who mentors students at Eagle Academy in the Bronx, likes to tell our students that as long as they're wearing the school uniform, conducting themselves like scholars with their pants pulled up (not sagging low in the prison style), the guys on the street will see what they're about. In my own experience, once we moved to Queens and were part of that large group of kids on the block, some pretty tough guys who would come into our neighborhood, but they didn't see us as part of what they were doing. Some days I would see one of these guys coming. Sometimes he spoke to me. I learned to talk to them respectfully—"Hey, how you doing"—but without any suggestion that I needed anything. And they would greet me and move on. I remember one guy in the area who had a frightening reputation, but in person, on an ordinary afternoon, he was soft-spoken. He would go his way and I would go mine.

Rules for safety, like preparation for emergency situations, are important, but they are not enough. If young people feel they are being restricted for no reason, they're going to rebel. If they feel they are missing out on life, they are going to seek excitement elsewhere. My friend Janice wouldn't have stayed on that porch forever, no matter how firmly her mother insisted. The kids on 223rd Street played on the block not just because that was the rule, but because we loved the things we could do there and the community we had formed. Our young men need us not only to set the limits that keep them safe, but also to make it worthwhile for them to stay within those limits.

Of course, parents can't do all that alone. When I was growing up, the parents on our block were always looking for worthwhile activities and sharing with each other what they found. One year, back in Brooklyn, I remember, my mother discovered a little museum called The Muse, just a short walk from where we lived, which offered free classes in photography and darkroom techniques. I had never seen a photograph develop in a tray of chemicals before, and I loved that. In the same way, Eagle school principals are constantly reaching out to local libraries, arts institutions, and businesses that can provide enriching activities for our young men. As my parents say, "There are blessings all around us." But they don't fall in your lap. You have to reach out to discover them.

In working to provide safe passage for our young men, we never feel we have all the answers. Young people change quickly, and all we can do is try to keep up. We ask ourselves: What are the dangers facing our young men *today*? How can we better prepare them to handle themselves wisely when they have to be in more risky environments? And how can we motivate and inspire them to use the preparation we have given them, at those crucial moments when we can't be there with them?

The answers change over time, and there are no guarantees, but returning frequently to the questions helps us to tip the odds in our children's favor.

CHAPTER THREE

YOUR FRIENDS OR YOUR LIFE

Exerting Positive Peer Pressure

On the spectrum of students who come to Eagle Academy, Charles Miller was at the far extreme, the kind of young man who could make almost anyone—parent, teacher, administrator, classmate—want to give up. Although he could be playful and silly, he was more often disruptive and violent. He prided himself on having more fights than any student at the school. Charles was already a gang member before he started with us in the ninth grade, and our basketball coach called him "the meanest, nastiest gangbanger in the Bronx as far as I was concerned. He was on a path to having a crew out there murdering people." When he was sent to a juvenile detention center in the middle of his years at Eagle, no one could have called it a surprise. Nor was it a surprise when he came back, tried to change his ways, and then after a few weeks went back to fighting and disrupting class. The surprise was that in his senior year, he had an increasingly strong feeling that he needed to graduate and go to college. It became a kind of mission for him, and an inspiration to all of us. There's a chance of getting through to even the most hardened young man.

Before starting his first year with us, Charles missed the Eagle summer orientation, Summer Bridge, but did attend the brief orientation in the fall, Summer Abridged, and participated in a college visit to Rutgers University. It was an eye-opening experience for him, "inspirational," he says. "We got to see all the different programs they had. I felt: *I want to go to college and when I do go to college I want to go here.*" It wasn't the first time Charles had a vision of himself with a positive future. For years he dreamed he would become a state trooper, until his prison record made that impossible. This new vision of himself at college could easily have gone the way of those other spoiled plans. But this time, he followed through.

What changed? Charles points to the feeling he developed, slowly, that he and his classmates were "brothers." At his previous schools, he says, "School was work, quizzes, tests, after-school programs—and then you go home. So I didn't expect high school to feel so family-oriented." At Eagle, the students call each other "bro," and the term takes on a singular importance. "It's different from when a regular person calls me 'bro.' I really considered Eagle students my brothers."

Along with the family feeling, what Charles calls the "brotherness," his Eagle brothers shared a set of expectations about success both as scholars and in the future. When Charles saw that his grades might be too low to graduate, this kid who was known as a tough guy felt afraid. "I was scared of not graduating, not going to college at the same time as everybody else," he says. "I didn't want to be one of *those* brothers, that ended up getting kicked out or just falling off."

That kind of positive peer pressure, rooted in what Charles called a "family feeling," is something we work to instill in our students, but the truth is that in our first year we were still learning how. Charles remembers being led through an unsuccessful trust exercise in which he had to wear a blindfold and fall back into a fellow student's waiting arms. He remembers thinking, *Why the ——— are we doing this? It takes a lot more than that to make trust!*

Charles began to feel some genuine trust when he befriended another ninth grader named Trevor, a "man-child" who seemed much taller and stronger than his years, with long dark braids. They both loved basketball, and they found they had something important in common: neither boy knew his mother. The boys rode the same city bus home from school, and Charles would "do dumb stuff on the bus"—harass another passenger, steal someone's electronic device, start a fight—"so we'd have something to talk about the next day."

For Charles, having something to talk about and someone to talk with was rare indeed. His mother had left the family by the time he was three. "It's like I've never seen her," Charles explains. "I have to imagine things based upon the words of my father. Sometimes I give up on imagining and it's easier to see her as a silhouette."

His father, a former boxer who worked seasonal jobs in construction and painting, was not a talkative man. "There was a big age difference, and he didn't really know how to connect with me. He just had directions he wanted me to follow. Even today, I've got to relate to him for us to have a connection. There's not much relating to me."

At Eagle, for the first time, he had friends to talk with, and by tenth grade, they were competing for success with girls. "Now it wasn't so much about impressing guys, it was about impressing females and getting the most. And then we'd talk about that on the bus the next day." The friends called themselves the 6 Bus Crew.

Harassing fellow bus passengers and competing for sexual conquests are not what any parent or teacher would hope for their ninth- or tenth-grade boy to do after school, but for Charles this was a rare chance to develop deep friendships. In time, he and Trevor started going out with two girls who were also friends. "Now you're double dating and everybody's getting closer," he says. Charles's sense of "brotherness" was growing. And when other members of the 6 Bus Crew started to get serious about graduating and going to college, Charles felt it was his responsibility, too—that's what his crew was doing.

Charles's grades were poor—"a lot of fifty-fives and below." He didn't have enough credits to graduate on time. He knew he had the option of returning for one more year at Eagle, but he didn't want to be "one of those brothers" who shows up to watch his own class graduate without him. So he enrolled himself in a GED class, a high school equivalency course for those who couldn't complete high school in the usual way. Many of those students were in the correctional system. "Now I was back among inmates and parolees." But those guys hadn't gone to Eagle! I got the highest score in the class!"

In terms of my expectations for students overall, this was not impressive. An equivalency degree carries a lot less weight than a high school degree, and it offered him a far more limited range of colleges to attend. But for Charles, this was a dramatic change in direction. He earned his high school equivalency degree and started taking college courses the next fall, on the same schedule as his peers. He had gotten back on the path to a productive life.

Charles's story illustrates a larger point about young men. Some are loners by choice, but most have a strong need to be a part of a bigger group. Just as teenage boys are going to range beyond the physical limits their parents set when they were children, they are going to range beyond their families and put their trust in a group of peers. In that group, they will compete with one another and make commitments to one another—and then take those commitments seriously, working to win the approval of their peers. For many, that group becomes the number one influence in their lives, more important than church or family. As parents or educators, we may like this change in our boys or we may not, but the change comes no matter what we feel and it will have an enormous influence on the success our young men do or do not achieve.

Few people understand this as clearly as Rashad Meade, principal of Eagle Academy in Brooklyn. Meade was born and raised in the Queensbridge housing projects, one of the largest and most dangerous housing developments in North America, and his environment, and the peer group it offered him, were nightmarish. In the 1980s and 1990s, during the height of the crack cocaine epidemic, he often smelled crack smoke in the elevator and in the hallway outside his apartment. Teachers from his local middle school came to his building to buy drugs, so his mother fought to have him moved to another school. "At first, when you see things like that, you experience a level of loss and shock," he says. "But by the time I was thirteen, many of my peers were making very easy money selling drugs. It didn't even seem like it was wrong."

Meade's closest friends were his teammates on the St. Rita's basketball team. "I didn't have a group of peers from my neighborhood all doing the right thing," he says. "Of the young men on the team with me, only one or two graduated from high school. I'm the only college graduate. One became a rapper. Many of the others went to prison. One did ten years for carjacking a parole officer. One did fifteen years for murder."

Meade was fortunate to have been raised by two devoted parents, both of whom worked to help him understand that the life he saw around him was not the only choice. His father especially helped him to use the negative influences all around them, the upside-down world where "doing well" for a thirteen-year-old meant selling drugs and carrying weapons, to fuel his son's desire for something better. While his mother fought for better opportunities for him, his father was his guide to the "safe passage" I described in the previous chapter, helping him understand that he faced two kinds of risks: that his peers might influence him to do something with serious consequences, and that it might be damaging enough just to be at the wrong place at the wrong time—sitting in a car with someone carrying drugs or weapons, for example, and getting stopped by the police.

To succeed, Meade discovered, he would have to make a terrible choice: to let go of all his high school friends, and start over in college with friends who did not pose the same dangers. When he did run into his old friends, he would tell them, "It's great seeing you," though he would be thinking: *I can't have you in my house. I can't drive you somewhere, because I don't know what you've got on you. I can't be around you for long.* The cost of safe passage was giving up his friends at the age when, emotionally, he needed them most.

Many young men couldn't have done it. Meade did, and the effort left him with a lifelong respect for the powerful influence of a young man's closest friends. That awareness was part of what drove him to work in education and to become an Eagle principal. "If we succeed at what we're attempting to do," he explains, "all of our young men will rise up with sixty or seventy peers who will have the same focus and drive." No one will have to make the brutal choice he faced: your friends or your life.

Instead, our young men will have an experience like I had growing up on 223rd Street. No one on that block asked, "Do you think you'll finish high school?" because finishing was what everyone expected of you—parents, neighbors, friends, everyone. We had peers with whom we could study, compete, let off steam, and celebrate. Similarly, we want our young men to have an experience like the kind you would take for granted at a private prep school: everyone is expected to go to college; and the peer pressure, that natural competitiveness, and the boyish camaraderie doesn't take away from that goal, they *add* to it. You know that if you advance in ways that others in your family did not, you won't be left alone. You're part of a group that shares those goals. You get to college and you find more peers like that. You pursue your future, and again, you have peers alongside you. All that youthful male energy, loyalty, and competitive drive is harnessed for the good.

BUILDING A BROTHERHOOD

Put young men together and you can be sure they will organize themselves into a social structure of some kind, just as Charles Miller and his friends from the 6 Bus Crew did on their rides home from school. When boys spend their days together, overcome adversity together, compete together, wear the same colors, pledge to look after each other in hard times, you can be sure they will develop a powerful loyalty. But loyalty in the service of what? Charles Miller and his friends forged their sense of belonging by starting fights and committing petty crimes. A gang with its colors and its rituals appeals to the same qualities in young men as does a great high school. For this reason, educators and parents can't be content to let the social structure evolve "naturally"—we may not like the result. Instead, we need to help our young men find situations where the brothers they find are brothers in success. They will make their own friends in their own ways, but we need to put them in situations where the bonds they will inevitably form will be, as much as possible, with young men who are moving in a positive direction. We need to help them recognize the dangers, and guide them in the choices they make. Just as we help them find safe passage through the physical streets where they live, it's up to us to help them find safe passage through their new social world.

At Eagle, we work from the first moments we are with our new students to build a brotherhood of scholars, fellow boys on the path to becoming good men. Some young men already have older siblings at home who can be a guiding brotherly or sisterly influence, but many either have no older siblings or they have negative influences. Some have involved fathers who can guide them as Rashad Meade's father guided him through the middle of the crack epidemic, but most don't. Some attended middle schools or other organized programs where they learned to support one another as they worked for positive goals, but again, most didn't. We realized that we had to be prepared to build a brotherhood among our students as if they had no other peer support, because for some, their Eagle brothers will be the only boyhood friends that they will ever have who are making constructive choices. As educators and parents, we must be prepared to do the same—establish a brotherhood.

FOSTERING BROTHERHOOD

There is no one blueprint for building positive fraternal feelings. At Eagle we have created what we call the house model. When our students are first accepted for sixth grade, they are assigned to one of several groups known as "houses" that are named after male role models of color: Roberto Clemente House, W. E. B. Dubois House, or Malcolm X House, for example. Some of our teachers have compared the houses to those in the *Harry Potter* series, others to the college fraternity system, but their defining quality is this: an Eagle rises and falls with his house, and the essential message of the house system is that our young men are part of a larger family, and that family has a stake in their well being, their development, and their future. Every student eats breakfast and lunch with the others in his house, and the boys participate in all extracurricular activities together. House brothers are teammates for intramural sports. His house brothers are the students that an Eagle knows best, who help him define who he is and meet the challenges of an Eagle education: when he stumbles, his house brothers are the first people he can turn to for support. In their activities, both academic and extracurricular, they gain or lose points together that we aggregate and display for all to see. When a student doesn't turn in his homework, his house loses between one and five points. When he succeeds, his house brothers will celebrate with him. And every time he gains or loses points for his house, we list his name along with those of his brothers for all to see.

Every year, when house assignments are given to our new Eagles, there are requests to switch to a house with a friend. The student will tell the principal, *"I want to switch. My mother is going to call. . . . "* But no Eagle has ever changed houses. We tell parents that we consider this a crucial way of teaching young men what family means. You're born into your family. You don't get to choose it. If a young man can accept the house he is given, grow to take care of his house brothers, and value the society they create together, then he is learning how to be a man. A man doesn't leave his family. A man takes care of his own. And an Eagle will learn to engage, respect, and love his house brothers.

In a typical school setting, students will sort themselves by social groups or by level of academic achievement—a young man struggling with a severe IEP might hang out with the other "special ed" students, while a high flier might find other academic stars. But everything in the house system is designed to build loyalty and teamwork across an array of types among the members of a house. In this way, we draw on their enthusiasm for competitive games and encourage a feeling of responsibility to the group to energize and focus their studies, not unlike the dynamics in team sports. Now they know that if they slack off, they will feel the wrath of their peers. If they skip a quiz or don't contribute in class, it will seem as if they do not care about the group. We set that up deliberately to put healthy peer pressure on the kids, so they will feel, in the terms that matter most to them, that they are responsible to one another. House points earn them special privileges and trips that they take together as a house if they win.

To support their success, we provide an hour and a half during each extended day for those who need it to do their homework in school. That way we eliminate the excuse of not having a quiet place to study at home, and provide staff supervision for those students who need a little more direction to do their homework. A student who still has incomplete homework by the end of the week gets a kind of detention on Fridays, when he has to stay, with tutorial support if he needs it, until his homework is done. In these ways we make not doing your homework almost a cardinal sin, and house brothers feel motivated to remind, encourage, and tutor one another to get their work done. This is especially important for quick, articulate young men, many of whom were smart enough to pass their tests in their old schools without studying. We use the motivation of the house system to help them realize that in our Academies, as in adult life, you have to do the work. We help them build a scholarly work ethic they may not have had before.

We start them on that journey with Summer Bridge. One new student, Dennis, recalls that on the first day, he was so nervous he couldn't eat breakfast. "That first morning they asked me my name and I was shy because I didn't know anybody. I didn't know what to expect besides strict teachers." A teacher lined up the students, then handed out blindfolds and asked each new student to put one on. Then the teacher told the boys to grasp the shoulder of the boy in front of them and walk forward. Each young man would follow the young man in front of him. Each one would lead the one behind him. The teacher said that if the boys took off their blindfolds or let go of the boy in front of them, they would be breaking the chain and putting themselves in danger. They might walk into walls or furniture, but if they held on to their brothers, they would be fine. He said, "In order to do this, you have to trust your brother."

Dennis found it "kind of scary" to walk without seeing, but he followed the young man ahead of him and when he took off his blindfold, he saw that they'd gone from one room to another, a place that was new to him. "At first I didn't know what was going on," he says. "Then they explained it and I understood. We're our brothers' keepers and we need to watch out for one another."

The young men were still frightened and hesitant to participate. As Shaun Neblett, a drama teacher who helped develop the first Summer Bridge program, explains, "They get embarrassed. There's a lot of nervous laughter. They're too scared to show a lot of dissidence or to be vocally combative with the staff, but you hear sly comments, laughter, a lot of looking around to see—*If he does it, I'll do it.*" At these moments, we begin to put peer pressure to positive use: now they are not just looking to one another for approval, but for permission to take positive risks.

In these early days we try to identify students who can help influence their new brothers to participate. We'll pick out one boy who is doing well early on, who has completed his first reading assignment but who also has some street swagger, and we'll declare him King for a Day. He'll get to wear a staff T-shirt instead of the Summer Bridge student T-shirt. The others then start to see that there are some rewards here in Summer Bridge, that this can be fun. You can be recognized—and in this age group, it's important that the recognition come right away. You can gain authority, and you can be valued in the eyes of your peers. It's the beginning of another Eagle promise: this is a place where we can help you develop, help you become a man.

BROTHERS IN THE UNIFORM

At the same time that we are offering some rewards for participating, we are also making clear some of the obligations and rules of the community. While the students are not yet required to wear a shirt, tie, and slacks, as they will be during the academic year, they have to wear the Summer Bridge T-shirt and it must be tucked into their jeans. From the beginning, we talk about the reasons behind the rules. We are not strict for the sake of being strict. We are trying to create a common ground where every Eagle can begin his journey on equal footing with his brothers. When they all wear T-shirts that match, we eliminate any competition over clothing. It reminds everyone that we are not here to evaluate one another based on how we look, but instead on the content of our character and our academic excellence.

We stress the importance of taking care of themselves and showing it in the way they present themselves to the world. We make sure every young man knows how to introduce himself by offering a firm handshake and looking the person he is meeting in the eye. We talk about how wrinkled clothes can make a young man seem like he doesn't care about himself. We teach the boys to use an iron. We talk about how dressing in the style inspired by prison clothing—no belt, sagging the pants—sends a message about how you see your own future. Of course, these ideas around grooming can be applied in any school and home setting whether or not a uniform is required. At Eagle, we let them know that when regular classes start in the fall, they can get detention for these uniform infractions. And though they may object to the uniform at times, all the young men will admit that, for better or worse, they are treated differently by strangers when they wear it. Adults are impressed. Young men are told they "look like gentlemen." Like it or not, the world takes them more seriously.

The reaction in their home neighborhoods isn't always positive. One Eagle described it this way: "If you're from the hood and you go to a uniform school, when you come home the kids you used to play with will crack jokes. They'll tease you, pull your chain." This taunting is designed to undermine their resolve. A shirt and tie means they're soft. If you're in school with boys all day, you'll "never get any girls." You "must be gay." These negative messages give us the chance to begin another important conversation with our students.

We tell them, "You Eagles can go out in the world and accomplish all sorts of things, and when you come back, those guys will still be there on the street corner, if they haven't gotten locked up or killed. You already know their future. You may not know yours but you know theirs. So, do you really want to listen to those guys?" We try to make the connections explicit: the uniform shows that they are part of this brotherhood. The brotherhood is there to help them achieve a better future. When they can wear it with pride, they won't mind some teasing on the street corner, because it reminds them of the future they're building for themselves.

The uniform is the most visible sign of a deeper lesson, about the power of personal accountability as students and young men. Many of our new Eagles have come from schools where there were no real consequences for arriving late or missing school entirely. They may not have been expected to complete their homework. They may never have felt what it is like to come unprepared to class and have a teacher ask a direct question they couldn't answer. Our students may tell each other that they enjoyed this apparent freedom, that their old school provided a chance to play under the radar, but for students, this lack of accountability, over time, is crippling. Jeff Levar, a former math teacher who for a time ran Summer Bridge in the Bronx, says that for many of these entering students, "Their spirits are broken. They feel like just passing is good enough. They feel: *if I fail, I'll just go to summer school and they'll pass me there.* They don't feel they can achieve. In Summer Bridge, we have to reverse that."

To help students become accountable, we have to hold them accountable, class hour after class hour, day after day. We have to show them that they have to do their homework, yes, every day, and that if they don't they are letting their brothers down. That they have to come to school on time, yes, every day, and again, if they don't they are letting their brothers down. That if they have more than two absences over the four weeks of Summer Bridge, they will be required to come back at the beginning of the school year for Summer Abridged. That the teachers know their names and care enough to follow their progress—many Eagle students discover, to their surprise, that if they act up in one class, the teacher of the next class will hear about it between classes and will be on the lookout for either a continuation of poor behavior or for improvement later in the day. They come to expect it. In all these small, practical ways, we contradict the low expectations they have of school. Through our consistency, we show them what education is supposed to be.

Of course, our goal is not just to have rule-abiding, presentable students. They came to us to learn. To understand how prepared they are, we first request students' academic records from their prior schools. Next, during days of Summer Bridge we do our own internal assessments of their skills in math and English language arts. Usually the two measures align, but sometimes we find that a student is much stronger than his grades would suggest. Once we have a clear sense of where they are starting out, we do as much individual instruction as possible. The teachers guiding the academic component of Summer Bridge are the same ones who will teach the incoming class, so Summer Bridge gives them the opportunity to get to know the needs of their incoming students right away. We hold individual meetings with parents in which we share the strengths and areas in need of improvement that we have observed. Often we will ask them to get specific books for a child to read over the summer, and make sure they are aware of ways to talk with their son about the extra work.

The larger goal of Summer Bridge is to get students ready to work harder than they've ever worked, albeit with the support of a dedicated staff and their new brothers. One of their first and most important experiences of intense individual effort, supported by the group, comes when we ask each student to memorize the poem "Invictus," by William Ernest Henley, and to practice it until they can recite it in unison. The poem begins:

Out of the night that covers me,
Black as the pit from pole to pole,
I thank whatever gods may be
For my unconquerable soul.

For our sixth graders, many of whom have read little poetry and may never have memorized a poem before, this is a demanding academic assignment. It takes time for them to understand Henley's description of reaching within oneself to endure pain and overcome hardship.

In the fell clutch of circumstance
I have not winced nor cried aloud.
Under the bludgeonings of chance
My head is bloody, but unbowed.

Later, students tell the story of memorizing the poem as if it were a difficult journey. The poem starts out easily enough, with two short lines, but after the second line the sentences get longer and harder to remember. Many students become afraid they can't memorize the whole thing at the required pace, one stanza a week for the four weeks of Summer Bridge. They work with their teachers on memorization strategies, such as breaking a long line into two pieces and memorizing one piece at a time. They practice in the evening at home with their families, keenly aware that all Eagle brothers will be lined up together to recite, and that if a teacher hears a brother who can't keep up recitation, the teacher will call the student out. We have a double message: first, that they are being invited to participate in something very special, and second, that they have serious responsibilities to shoulder if they are going to be part of it. As one sixth grader put it, "If I didn't do it, I wouldn't have been able to share this moment with everyone. I would have been the rotten apple."

Memorizing "Invictus" gives our new Eagles an initial experience overcoming a tough academic challenge individually, but in the company of their Eagle brothers who faced the exact same challenge and fears. Once they learn it, reciting it together as they will do often during their years at Eagle, becomes a ritual that brings them closer to the group, like singing a school alma mater or a team's fight song. The words of the poem express the commitments the students are making with their brothers to take charge of their own lives and re-invent their futures as young men, no matter what the obstacles—a reminder of why Eagles believe in themselves, of what this brother-hood stands for.

> *It matters not how strait the gate,*
> *How charged with punishments the scroll.*
> *I am the master of my fate:*
> *I am the captain of my soul.*

"Invictus" sets the bar very high for our young men. It tells them that whatever challenges they may face in their families, their neigh-borhoods, or their nation, they can be the masters of their fate, the authors of their own futures.

STEPPING UP

At the end of four weeks, the culmination of Summer Bridge is what we call the Stepping Up ceremony. The students gather with their parents and the Summer Bridge staff. Many are excited for the parents to meet the teachers they have been hearing about for the past month. Parents tell the teachers about their sons coming home eager to read, or talking nonstop about events at school, some for the first time in their lives. The students recite "Invictus" all together in one loud voice. They offer performances, readings, and songs they have worked on over the past four weeks. They perform a ceremony of gratitude in which every student thanks those who helped him meet the challenges he faced. Before they are formally invited to come back in September as Eagle students, they are presented with their freshman ties. Many have never worn a tie before, and a family member ties the tie for them. The whole assembled group witnesses this gathering of young men who've come together in a very short period of time in a spirit of brotherhood.

A few years ago, I had a superintendant of schools from the Midwest visit on the day of the Stepping Up ceremony. When he arrived that morning, he was full of questions about our curriculum and our pedagogical methods. I answered his questions, but I kept encouraging him to stay for the ceremony. He agreed, and he heard one young man read a composition, thanking his mom for all that she had done for him. He was a big kid, and to hear him pour out his feelings was very special. There was not a dry eye in the house. His mother came up to the stage afterward, hugging him and crying. I told the superintendant that a lot of young men would not be that comfortable sharing this in front of his peers had they not gone through the kind of positive peer-bonding experience we provide our young men. And he said, "Now I get it. This is not necessarily about your curriculum. You've created a social ethos and that's what makes Eagle special. What you've got is a spirit. That's the magic."

Of course, as I've described, there is a great deal of practical evaluation and instruction in Summer Bridge. By the end, the students are ready to get to work—they have a basic academic grounding in math and English language arts, they have developed a sense of study skills and their responsibilities as students, and they know what will be expected of them, both inside and outside the classroom. But just as important, or probably more important, is that by the end of Summer Bridge they are happy because they have gained relationships with the adults in school and with their Eagle brothers, and they feel they will be able to rely on those relationships when school starts. You can see when you look around at the Stepping Up ceremony that the young men are relaxed and affectionate with each other. They aren't engaging in the tough posturing you will see on the street corner, or even in many high school hallways. They feel secure because they have a house. They have brothers. They belong.

GOOD THAT FEEDS ON ITSELF

Two remarkable things happen when young men start to feel loyalty to peers who share their positive goals and commitments. The first shows how a spirit of brotherhood can be such a strong force for success, and the second shows why this profound resource often gets lost or goes unappreciated.

If you eavesdrop a little on Eagle brothers when they're together, you'll overhear moments of brothers supporting brothers, where one encourages another who is feeling down, reinforcing the lessons from teachers and pushing him toward success in their own boy-ways. A lot of that happens without our knowing it. In chapter six, I describe the Eagle approach to mentoring and its crucial impact on the lives of our young men, but even the most dedicated mentor is only with our students a few hours a month. The success of our mentoring depends on the young men internalizing what the mentors say and passing it on to their Eagle brothers. It's not just that brothers reinforce what the mentors and staff are doing—in many cases, what the students say to one another is more powerful than what they hear from adults. No inspiring speech from the principal about how they belong and how at Eagle they will be lifted when they fall can compare to the feeling of getting help from your peers when you need it.

But the more the spirit of brotherhood works, the less visible it becomes. Kids always develop their own language and their own ways of conveying values among themselves, and when it's harmful, adults often rail against it, wishing that our young people were less influenced by what their peers say and do. But as positive peer pressure develops, and students get into less trouble, the teaching staff and the parents at home don't have to intervene as much. Many excellent teachers, who can spot students who are strong academically, can't see that weak students are sometimes the strongest leaders, able to influence the entire class to move in the right direction. Teachers see the successes and celebrate them with the students, but don't always see the mechanism by which a near failure became a triumph thanks to brotherly leadership and resilience. Often teachers and administrators alike don't know which student stepped in to help, or who set an example without even knowing a younger Eagle was watching him and taking it in.

I was reminded of this when I spoke to our former student Roberto Huie after he graduated from Eagle Academy and started at West Point—our first Eagle ever to go to West Point. I asked him which house he had belonged to, and at first he couldn't remember. Was that proof that the house system hadn't mattered to him? As he recalled his experience of "brotherhood," I realized it was the opposite, proof of just how powerful his membership in a brotherhood had been.

Roberto grew up in the Bronx in what he calls a "bad neighborhood," close to gang activity, drug abuse, and a feeling among kids his age that school wasn't something you needed to care about. Quiet and a little awkward, he was often teased about his big ears. But at his middle school he was mentored by a teacher who wanted to replicate the mentoring he had experienced himself in the fraternity Kappa Alpha Psi, in which brothers were mentored by graduates, then graduated and came back to mentor students. That teacher became the school's assistant principal, and Roberto was fortunate to be there when he implemented the new program, starting late in seventh grade and continuing to eighth grade. As a result, by the time he was twelve, Roberto already had a group of brothers—"before I got myself in any trouble." They played basketball together, studied together, and competed for grades together. They were brothers in success. Several came to Eagle together, and brought that same family feeling with them.

At that time, the Eagle house system, which had originated in our Brooklyn school, was not yet in place in the Bronx. By the time he was assigned to a house, Roberto was a senior, deep in the college application process. But he already had his brotherhood. Unlike Charles Miller, who needed a couple of years before the family feeling became strong enough to guide him toward graduation and college, Roberto had it from day one. So when our college counselor, Donald Ruff, started making our students aware of summer programs on college campuses where high school students could earn college credits, Roberto not only knew he was interested, but had Eagle brothers for moral support during the application process and even on campus.

Roberto had the benefit of a brotherhood of success from early on, so much so that it became something expected. Charles Miller, though he also benefited, came to it much later, and missed some of the opportunities Eagle offered. With perseverance, Charles earned his high school equivalency degree, a triumph for him. But he still feels, "If I had a time machine and I could go back and listen to every piece of advice from Eagle, I would. If I could put it all on a memory card and implement that in my own past, I would. I think my life would be better than what it is now just as a result of that."

A CONSPIRACY OF CARE

For parents and anyone else who takes responsibility for young men, its essential to remember that when you are choosing activities for young people, or allowing them to choose how they will spend their time, you are also helping to select the peers who will influence them so deeply. Young men need adult help in finding positive peer groups, and it won't be enough just to say no to "bad influences." Our young men need to be actively directed toward more positive influences, and put in situations where they can discover for themselves the pleasure of having friends and fellow competitors on the path to achievement. For families not finding positive peers at school, it will be all the more important to seek advice and support from other parents, teachers, coaches, and other adults in a young man's life. Nothing is more likely to get another parent's attention than to say, "You've got a great young man there. I'd love for our kids to spend more time together." Similarly, any coach, teacher, camp counselor, or faith leader who cares for young men would love to be told, "What you are doing here is exactly what I want for my son. I see how you bring out the best in these kids. Do you have any idea of how we can keep this going, even when they're not with you?" The goal is to put together what my good friend and mentor, Ron Walker, executive director of the Coalition of Schools Educating Boys of Color, calls a "conspiracy of care": adults and families who want to help young men bring out the best in each other, so that the powerful forces of peer influence and peer pressure can be put to the best possible use.

CHAPTER FOUR

BEYOND CHALK AND TALK

Reaching Young Men in the Classroom

When we picked Karla Chiluiza to teach algebra at Eagle Academy, she wasn't an obvious choice. Slight, soft-spoken, hesitant to raise her voice, Ms. Chiluiza was twenty-two years old and only recently certified to teach—a rookie facing a room full of ninth-grade boys for the first time. And what a group of boys! That first year, by the time we'd gotten the green light to open Eagle Academy, we had already missed the regular Department of Education "selection" process, in which most New York middle-school graduates choose the high schools they want to attend. So we wound up with a significant population of young men with serious social, emotional, and academic challenges, roughly three-quarters of whom were reading below their grade level.

What was Ms. Chiluiza doing there at the front of that demanding classroom? A graduate of an all-girls school, she had worked as a student teacher at Young Women's Leadership Academy and had become passionate about single-gender education. She had also grown up on 167th Street and the Grand Concourse in the Bronx, just blocks from our first school building; this job was her chance to bring her deep commitment to single-gender education back home.

She spoke every day about the upcoming Regents exam, reminding her students that they would be facing the test required by New York State so they would have a practical reason to get down to work. She handed out algebra tiles to make the abstractions of math more hands-on. She passed out graphing calculators, hoping to engage the boys with technology. But some of the students treated their algebra tiles as toys, throwing them around the room. They liked working with the calculators, but one student used his to hit a classmate in the face. Such interruptions made it hard to carry on teaching.

Ms. Chiluiza had arrived inspired to be part of a new all-boys school, but her class quickly became a disaster. The boys were energetic and restless, and they engaged in almost constant disruptive behavior, ignoring her, horsing around, and refusing to do the work she assigned. In small-group work sessions, Charles Miller, the little Caesar, started fights. Ms. Chiluiza was spending most of her time trying to get her class to *begin* learning. "It seemed to me that nothing I did was working," she says. "I didn't seem to be reaching them at all. It was the hardest thing I've ever done."

CAN YOU CONTROL BOYS?

There were larger reasons that things went so badly in Ms. Chiluiza's class. That first year, Eagle didn't yet have its legs underneath it—our culture and rituals were still being developed. The students were all ninth graders that first year, with no older students to model the Eagle way for their younger brothers and help keep them in line.

But as understandable as some of Ms. Chiluiza's obstacles may have been, there were deeper doubts that emerged. Visitors to the school would often ask, "How can you keep control of boys like that? How can you even begin to teach them? What do you do with boys who won't listen and won't learn?" I've heard those questions many times, and I know what they imply: Can these boys be taught at all? Or are they somehow defective—hopeless? Most people, maybe even most educators, believe that the most challenging young men will be impossible to teach unless someone discovers a brave new world of radical approaches—special disciplinary methods and new pedagogical theories to use with young men of color, this category for which the normal educational rules might seem not to apply.

Ms. Chiluiza was using everything she had learned about teaching boys, and going frequently to the more experienced teachers and to me for advice. But nothing worked. Was it time to give up?

At the end of her unsuccessful first year, we offered her three options: she could leave Eagle entirely; she could stay with us at Eagle and start over with the new, presumably easier, entering ninth-grade class; or she could pick up with those same students who had proven so challenging in the fall and try again.

"I remember thinking that summer," Ms. Chiluiza says, "that if I leave, my memories will be mostly negative memories." In a way, what she was feeling at her lowest—that it was hopeless with this group, that they would never succeed—was what the boys felt about themselves. Many of them had failed math in the past. Many expected that going to a public school in a poor neighborhood meant that the teachers would give up on you, and then promote you to the next grade so they wouldn't have to deal with you anymore. She decided, "I can't give up on the boys that way. I can't give up on myself. I need to stay with the group I started with and figure out how to connect with them."

On the first day of class that fall, her students were shocked to see her. "You didn't leave!" they called out. "I thought for sure you'd go!"

She said "No, I'm not going anywhere."

One boy after another expressed his surprise.

"She didn't leave!"

"Huh."

"You're still around!"

She told them, "I have you and you have me. That's all we have here. And there is still a Regents exam to pass—remember that?"

Ms. Chiluiza set to work again, trying to turn that class around with the approach she had planned over the summer, on her own and in conversation with other Eagle teachers and staff. Her plan was to sit down with her students one on one, so she could begin to understand what was going wrong for each of them individually. What was it about math that made this difficult for these boys? What was it about their lives that made it difficult for them to study and to conduct themselves as scholars in class? What was it about their families that she didn't know, but needed to know?

A lot of this work happened outside the regular class meetings. School would end and boys would come back to her classroom. She would talk to them. Then she would call home to get the parents' perspective on their son's progress, and to engage the parents more fully in their son's work. These were calls home about academic problems and disciplinary issues, what she called "daily conversations," checking in, so she and the parents could get to know one another. Ms. Chiluiza kept notes on all of the conversations she had with families, and in a year she filled three thick notebooks.

Once phone calls home became part of the regular teaching routine, she needed to be able to do something more when a more serious problem presented itself. In cases of serious disruption of class, she would ask a parent to come to school for a meeting. With all of these personal contacts, she began to discover what she called "the individual journeys" her students were taking. For many, math in particular was an old struggle, a history of failure and humiliation. Math had hurt them before and was likely to hurt them again. When they interrupted her teaching, she came to realize, they were not just boys being boys and they were not simply giving her attitude. They were distracting the class to avoid a familiar pain.

For Charles Miller, there wasn't a question of whether he was smart enough to complete the work. He was not applying himself, and intentionally so—he had tried applying himself in the past, it had ended badly, and he had given that up. Like my brother Philip, who stopped trying to compete with me for good grades, Charles was a highly energetic boy who had long ago stopped trying to compete as a scholar. He felt safer competing to be the class tough guy or the class clown.

Getting to know her students personally reinforced Ms. Chiluiza's sense that their bad behavior was not in their essential nature. Nor was it something directed at her—which meant that she didn't have to be afraid of it. It was, instead, an expression of their own fear that they would fail once again.

If a student continued to disrupt class, even after a parent meeting, she would call his parents or guardian to attend class with him, sitting in and participating in the lesson with the disruptive child and the rest of the students. In this way she hoped to demonstrate to all of the students: *Your family supports me in what we're trying to do here. They love you that much, and they are committed to the same high expectations I have for you, that you can succeed. We all believe you can do this.*

Not all of the conversations Ms. Chiluiza had with students and parents were about algebra or its challenges. Talking to these young men, she found that many were in a lot of pain. She marveled that some of them could get out of bed in the morning and go to school. Even some of the academically successful kids were living with serious dysfunction, in their families or their neighborhoods, but they were managing the dysfunction better than their peers who were struggling. This was beyond her expertise, but she had a support team she could turn to, including the guidance counselor, social worker, parent coordinator, and others on the staff who could help students find resources for dealing with outside issues. That team helped figure out whether the student could be served within the school or whether he needed to be referred to an outside organization. They could offer the parents referrals for their own counseling. The result was a real coming together to send a message to the kid: we care, and we are here to try to help.

Most Eagle students are not from dysfunctional families. Many come in like sponges, ready to soak up learning, ready to transform. Ms. Chiluiza had to learn where each student was starting from, how close to the starting line of the race. Some were already at the line, waiting for the starting gun. Some needed her help getting up to the starting line. Some had no sneakers. She met each student where he was so he could get ready to run the race.

In the second year, approaching her relationships with the boys in this new way, Ms. Chiluiza was able to establish a culture of learning in her classroom where none had existed before. She doesn't attribute the change to better classroom techniques or improved methods of discipline. "Something happened between 'the two of us'—me and the boys. We were able to finally support each other. I knew what they needed me to be. And that then created the kind of behavior in the classroom that allowed me to teach. We were able to find unison," she says.

In this new relationship with the young men, she was able to teach, and the class became dramatically more productive. In the spring, 94 percent of her original students passed the state's Regents exam in algebra.

That success filled the class with excitement and energy. Ms. Chiluiza began working with the science teacher to create a unit on bridge design through the lenses of both geometry and engineering. The classes took field trips to walk the bridges near the school, including the George Washington Bridge and the Brooklyn Bridge, and then the boys designed and built their own model bridges using Popsicle sticks. For their final projects, they displayed their bridges in the school's first math and science fair. One boy built a cantilever bridge, with a long span suspended in the air, like the Tappan Zee Bridge in New York State. Another student, Tyrell, built a suspension bridge. A few years later, Ms. Chiluiza ran into Tyrell coming out of the subway station in her neighborhood.

"I heard him call my name," she says. "He told me he was getting home from Lehman College, where he was studying accounting. He said, 'I want to thank you because you helped me understand math so when I got to college I wasn't afraid to take math or take accounting.'" She keeps that suspension bridge displayed in her home as a reminder of the work those challenging boys did their second year. "That was the foundation," she says, "from which I learned how to teach—and what it meant to be a teacher."

THE SUBJECT IS YOUNG MEN

Part of what made Ms. Chiluiza so successful that second year, and part of what we look for whenever we are hiring teachers and other staff members at Eagle Academy, was her deep understanding of the essential job qualification—not just to teach a subject such as math or social studies, but to teach it to young men. The job is *teaching young men*. Whenever I interview a potential teacher, and whenever I'm approached for advice about teachers who can succeed with the most challenging boys, I ask myself, Does this person have a specific commitment to working with boys? Will they be able to fit into a school culture that can deal with boys?

That might sound obvious, but even for me, the reality can take some getting used to. I remember one afternoon in my first year as the principal of Eagle Academy in the Bronx—my first year, that is, in an all-boys school. I was sitting at my desk when a student came tearing down the hall, running past my office door at top speed. Two seconds later, another boy ran by almost as fast as the first. Something was going on.

I had always taken pride in my ability to sense student conflict before it exploded, my feel for when a fight would break out, so I jumped up from my desk and ran to the door. Stepping into the hallway, I saw two boys on the ground locked in what looked like a death grip.

"What are you guys doing?!" I yelled.

They held on. I yelled even louder, running toward them now, wondering how bad it was going to get. When I was standing right above them, they both kind of rolled over together and looked up at me, neither one willing to let go.

"What?" asked one of them, smiling.

"We're just playing!" said the other.

They lay there looking up at me, grinning like I was the one acting crazy. This was no fight! They were goofing off. Their behavior was not appropriate, but neither was it a crisis. They didn't need the full authority of the school principal charging down the hall screaming to prevent mayhem. I thought to myself, *This is different from the co-ed situation I had before.*

Despite my own experience raising sons and my years in co-ed schools, I wasn't fully ready in a practical way for how boys play, especially when there are no girls around—roughhousing, horse-playing, slapping each other in the head, and carrying on in all sorts of startling physical ways. It's juvenile, it's silly, but for a while in their lives, that's precisely how they communicate.

That's why we need our teachers and other staff members to know the difference between boyish play that is inappropriate at school and needs to be redirected, like that wrestling match outside my office, and dangerous behavior that needs to be punished. When it's the former, we need to react firmly, but with understanding—not with anger or fear, throwing up our hands and saying, "Oh my God, what can we do about them?!" We need teachers and staff members who know that this behavior doesn't mean these young men are thugs or miscreants. It means they are boys.

We have found that, beyond any formal educational training, the teachers who have the deepest personal knowledge of how to guide young men often learned it from personal experience. When we interview candidates for a position at Eagle, we ask directly, "Do you have any boys? Do you have any brothers? Why do you want to work in an all-boys school? A classroom full of young men will test you. What draws you to that?" I remember one candidate, an experienced teacher, answered, "Oh, is this an all-boys school?" He had no idea. He was just a teacher looking for his next job, and though he might have been qualified in ordinary terms, he had no business teaching at a school for young men.

Having lived around boys is no guarantee, but if a candidate has three sons, a lot of the time he or she will get it. A female applicant who can say, "I was a tomboy, I had to keep up with two brothers," may well have a deeper understanding than that of many male teachers, an understanding that no formal training about gender and education can match.

NO FEAR

One of the worst teachers we ever had at Eagle was a big, strong man, qualified in every way you could measure on a résumé, but afraid of the boys. A student of ours finally said to him, out loud in front of others, "Mr. So-and-so, you act like you're scared of us."

He said, "Many of you, the way you act, I *am* afraid!"

With that, he was finished as a teacher at our school. There was nothing I could do to help him recover. At a moment like that, students are almost like sharks—when they smell blood in the water, when they sense that fear, that weakness, they lose respect.

But it's not a matter of acting tough to win their respect. Teenage boys discover quickly that even some adults are frightened of them, and what they won't tell you is that they find that fear frightening. As they grow, becoming more physically powerful and more outlandish in their behavior, they may begin to worry that no one can handle them. I spoke in the previous chapter about the need for parents to provide love, high expectations, and security, but there is an additional kind of security boys need from their teachers. That is security from themselves and their own destructive impulses and fears, and this is true of all boys, no matter what zip code they live in.

One of our students who could be a hell-raiser in class found a teacher who could stand up to him—and that made it possible for him to succeed. He tells the story this way:

"If a teacher is in the front of the class, and I'm being disruptive, and he takes the time to come all the way to my side of the room to tell me to cut it out, then he has lost the attention of everyone else. Everyone else is missing out because he focused on me. When I see a teacher put one disruptive person over everybody else, I lose confidence in him.

"Now, this history teacher had an accent. He was from the [Caribbean] islands. I would make fun of it, imitate it. Other guys would laugh and the teacher would realize what was going on. The first day I made fun of his accent, I got detention. A day or two later it happened again. I would act out and each time he would give me detention. So there comes a day in his class when I'm starting to do something dumb, and I see him start to get agitated, so I think to myself, *I don't want to get detention—stop it right now!*

"That's when I realized he was smart. I started to think, yo, I like that. He knows that we need this class more than he does. When you see someone is not going to waste their time for your bullshit, you start to value your time more—if he's not going to waste it, then I'm not going to waste it.

"Then we got cool, the two of us. We would talk about how life in the islands is different and how American kids take a lot of things for granted. I started participating more in class, answering questions, being in the spotlight academically instead of acting out. I wanted to show him I wasn't stupid—I wanted to show him I was smart."

When I hear an inspiring story like that—and I've heard many—it tells me that not allowing young men to act up is a form of caring. When teachers show young men that we aren't going to let them act up on our watch, that we have the understanding to stop them when they get out of line, that we care enough about their success to give them our all in the classroom, we show them they are safe with us. It may sound tough, but underneath it are still love, security, and high expectations.

FINDING YOUR PLACE

Graham still remembers his average from freshman year: 63.7. He came from a solid family with a mother and a stepfather, and, like his older brother, he had an intellectual appearance, neatly groomed with glasses. His older brother had been an academic star in high school and was now in college, but Graham struggled. He talked back to his teachers, refused to study, and made it clear to anyone who would listen what he thought school had to offer: nothing. His passion was hip-hop music, and he idolized the street life portrayed in the songs he loved. He was not a violent young man, but he could easily have failed out of school and found himself with some terribly narrow possibilities. I hate to see a smart young man, someone with the potential to earn a college degree and professional success, miss his chance and wind up working in a fast-food restaurant or a drugstore all of his life, maybe one day getting promoted to manager.

I used to talk to Graham about his potential. I told him, repeatedly, "You're an Eagle, so look up—the sky's the limit!" But the key was his sophomore year, when two teachers connected with him. His drama teacher recognized that music was Graham's calling, and he encouraged him to explore that calling in school, not just outside. Graham founded a hip-hop group in school with other Eagle students. Meanwhile, the debate teacher discovered another use for his smart-guy mouth: competing on the debate team. Graham still had his love of hip-hop and his smart mouth, but those two teachers helped him find places within the community for them. For the first time, Graham saw a chance to be true to himself and still be a success at school. He began to think of himself as an Eagle, and not just as a rebellious outsider. His grades began to improve. He had known from the beginning that other people thought he could succeed like his older brother, but now he began to see for himself how those expectations could apply to him, personally.

TEACHING FROM LOVE

If there is one thing that connects all that I believe we need to do for our young men, it's this: don't give up. Our students expect teachers and other authority figures to give up on them, and they have finely tuned antennae for sensing when an adult is only going through the motions. They are painfully sensitive to people going in and out of their lives, and they need teachers who are committed to how important that feeling is. What they respond to best is teachers who, like Ms. Chiluiza, stay with them, almost like family, with a devotion borne of, if not love, then at least a deep caring.

Some people would argue that a teacher cannot teach a student without some feeling of love for that student. I'm not saying teachers must love all their students, but to succeed with young men teachers must be willing to dedicate themselves, to give their all. Teachers who get through to their students have to want in a passionate way to make a difference in their students' lives. That's the nature of this work with young men. Teachers who don't have that dedication, that calling, should probably work with other, less emotionally vulnerable student populations. As Yvette Crespo, director of admissions, puts it, "You either love this work or it will consume you. I love this place. This is not a job for me; it's more like a calling. I believe there was a purpose and a reason that I came here." Aaron Barnette, the dean of students at Eagle Academy in the Bronx, says, "There are some days I come home and I'm real tired from doing this job. But it is what it is. I wouldn't choose anything else. I truly love this place. Even if I hit the lottery, I'd come in. I bleed Eagle Academy."

At Eagle Academy in Brooklyn, after four years, the school still had one hundred percent of its original staff. The awareness of that level of commitment all around them can make the difference for students who are afraid to trust in a school. Principal Meade explains, "That consistency helps young men see what we mean when we say Eagle is a family."

HOW YOUNG MEN LEARN

I have written so much here about teachers getting to know students individually and teaching from a dedication like love, that it might seem as if I think good teaching is a matter of emotional connection, not practical pedagogy to build practical skills. That isn't the case. The last thing that I want is to help produce a generation of young men who feel loved and safe—who feel, deep down, just plain great about themselves—but are skill deficient. At Eagle, we might be able to build our students up emotionally while they are with us, but if that is all we do, the depth to which they will fall is going to be very low indeed when they move on to college or employment and find they are not all we said they were. None of us can settle for Eagles with no wings!

I have emphasized security and dedication because our students, like all of us, need that foundation, just as a builder lays a foundation before constructing the rest of the building. Once young men have that secure emotional base, then like Karla Chiluiza's students in their second year, they are ready to make use of every approach that the pedagogical research has shown to engage and benefit young men. These include:

- Frequent talk about goals—"We have a Regents exam to pass, so you can get your diplomas"—to motivate young men with a sense of mission.
- Clear, personalized incentives, by the hour, the day, the week, and the year, to keep them progressing from step to step and goal to goal.
- Hands-on work related to real-world problems, to balance out the abstraction of more traditional "chalk and talk."
- School days and class hours structured to help them complete their work and keep away from distractions.
- Competitive learning games to fuel their motivation, in which teachers can present themselves as coaches helping their students to win.
- Cross-disciplinary studies that let them see the real-life impact of what they learn.
- A consistently increasing pace, compared to typical public high schools, to move students smoothly from remediation to accelerated learning.

Below, I say more about approaches to teaching young men, and show how they are parts of a larger whole.

OFFER INCENTIVES

When Eagle Academy in the Bronx was new, we found that for technical reasons, it was necessary to have our students eat lunch late, past one in the afternoon. But that awkward scheduling led to a discovery: our young men were far more successful in the classes they took before lunch than after. Lessons learned before lunch were often mastered in one try; lessons learned afterward too often needed to be retaught. We realized that our late lunch schedule was a disadvantage that could be turned into an advantage.

Now the entire Eagle school day is structured as an incentive to succeed academically. Most of our core academic classes, such as social studies, math, science, and English and language arts, meet between 9:00 a.m. and 1:20 p.m., when our young men's concentration seems to be best. We start the day with our most demanding requirements, and then follow the hard work with a satisfying reward: the sports and other activities they naturally enjoy. The same rule we encourage our parents to apply at home—take care of your business, then you can go play—shapes our extended school day.

This approach works best when we can fine-tune our rewards to satisfy each individual student. Many of our students come to school looking forward to the chance to play sports. Others are fired up for theater or robotics or culinary arts. For younger students, the sixth to eighth graders, a big reward at the end of the day is the chance to use the video-game room. There is one threshold for completed work just to get into the room and watch, and a higher threshold of performance to get to play. To our students, this is highly motivating—they want to get in there, show off their skills, compete with their friends—and a lot of homework gets done in study periods so that our younger students can get into that room. We skip the entire argument that pits "bad" video games against "good" learning, and use the incentives we have to boost their performance as scholars.

As they get older, we find we have to diversify the experiences we offer them as rewards. The video-game room is no longer the end-all and be-all. Some of the older boys would rather condition for lacrosse practice. Some want to have experiences that are more adventurous. In Brooklyn, we offer the eighth graders food trips, such as a Mexican buffet. Put food in front of boys and—clear the way! They appreciate it as something different, a new experience, and something the younger kids haven't earned. They don't want to miss out.

We have also tried a system we called Eagle bucks—play money you earn based on grades and behavior. Each "bill" featured a picture of someone from African-American or Latino history. So there was a little learning even as they were rewarded, and then they could redeem their Eagle bucks for prizes that they chose for themselves at the school store. That way we knew the reward would have personal value to them.

NOTHING GIVEN, EVERYTHING EARNED

What we want all the boys to discover, from the student-athletes to the student-gamers to the student-chefs, is that whatever comes after the hyphen, being a student comes first. Sports, arts, video games, other pleasures and rewards—these are privileges, not rights; they're not simply given, but earned. We make it our business to offer our students rewards that feel worth earning. Our basketball season is not two months long, it's eight months, because when our young men have the privilege of competitive basketball to lose, even those who haven't found their love of reading can be motivated to finish reading their books.

I am sometimes asked: Don't you care about intrinsic motivation? Shouldn't students be moved by a love of learning, rather than a promise of video games at the end of the day? And my answer is yes, but young men who have been failed by schools in the past have not had the chance to build up this feeling for the intrinsic worth of education. They may come to love it, but many of them don't love it yet. Education has been more like a torment they were required to endure. So we need something to get them feeling positively about it.

Part of the trouble is that many don't have the skills they would need in order to succeed enough to enjoy it. It's no good to be invited to a pool party if you can't swim. We face this dilemma every year around reading—we welcome many articulate, intelligent sixth grade boys who nevertheless read only at the third grade level. How can that be? In New York City elementary schools, students receive an enormous amount of test-taking preparation and they learn how to get by on a state exam, but when they face more substantial challenges—to write an original research paper, pass the English Regents, or write an essay for college admissions—these young men hit a wall. They know how to mark the right answers on a standardized reading test, but they don't, in a deeper sense, know how to read.

We change the focus back from testing to skills. We work on the foundations of reading and writing until our young men can articulate their thoughts on the fly in a clear, concise manner. These are very difficult skills for anyone, and for our students to succeed they have to grow two grade levels a year until they catch up.

We make reading a top priority. That means our students read in every class. They write in every class. Every teacher is made aware of that larger goal, even if he or she must sacrifice components of their individual class plan. We try to keep class sizes small. (The New York City Department of Education allows classes as large as thirty-two students, but we find that the energy and physical size of a class of thirty-two boys, especially when they're uncomfortable with a subject matter that has embarrassed them in the past, can feel more like fifty boys.) We try to limit our classes to twenty-two, even though that takes resources away from other commitments. We have a full-time reading specialist. Our goal is for our teachers to know exactly which students need to develop their reading skills, and to take their students' success personally. And we evaluate our reading teachers based on the progress their students make.

At the same time, we recognize that merely *scheduling* our students to spend more time on reading will make them neither like it nor excel at it. What will make them passionate readers, motivated by their own inner love of learning and exploring the world through writing? At first, honestly, nothing. Reading can be an essential tool and a lifelong love, but building the skills of reading is not something all students enjoy, especially if their past failure to master those skills has been a shame they've hidden for years. So to build the skills in our extended day and Saturday sessions, we start by building enthusiasm and familiarity. We make subject matter the incentive to keep practicing, and let our students read whatever interests them, including books you might not typically find in the curriculum of a co-ed school. Not all boys have the same tastes, but many choose stories of adventure, horror, and violent action. They choose a lot of graphic novels. (Mothers will often ask, "Is my son reading a comic book?" A teacher might answer, "Yes, one with the same literary themes as *The Great Gatsby*." When the kids start to dig into those graphic novels and we can't keep them on the shelves, then the parents see the value.) As they build the skills and habits of readers, a love of reading can take over, and we venture into more traditional literature. In this way, young men for whom reading was an embarrassing failure start to build success.

IT'S ALL EDUCATION

We also look for chances to show our students that whatever they work at, whether being an athlete, an actor, or a gamer, is learning. If they have a setback and they pick themselves up again and overcome it, we can say to them, "I saw you fall down on the court," or "I heard when you forgot the lines of that spoken-word piece," or "I remember when you lost your final life in that video game, right before you leveled up—and I saw how you kept at it and overcame that setback. That was resilience, and it's in your character when you're doing your algebra homework just as much as any other time. You can do that in your academics, too."

STRUCTURE: NO IDLE TIME

Just as we structure the days according to when our young men are better focused and to reward them for putting their academics first, we structure each individual class hour to do the same thing. Every hour, just like every day, we want them to understand the mission they share and take care of their business first. In every class, every day, students arrive to find that the teacher has put a "Do Now" problem or exercise on the board. While this is a common beginning for a class meeting in many schools, at Eagle our teachers tell their students exactly the protocol they expect:

- Line up outside of your classroom and enter in an organized way, to show that you are prepared to work.
- Go straight to your seat and read the "Do Now" assignment on the blackboard.
- Complete that assignment—which will be graded and counts toward the class participation requirement—within five minutes.

This high degree of structure, with a clear goal, a set time frame, and a clear reward, keeps our students motivated and prevents idle time. If they don't get lost in those shapeless, unsupervised first few minutes of class, they don't have time to begin a distracting conversation, get out their cell phones, grow preoccupied with the view out the window, or start a conflict with their classmate. They don't have the time to go wrong. The structure of the class hour helps them to take care of their business first.

As Aaron Barnette, dean of Eagle Academy in the Bronx, explains, "Behavioral difficulties happen when there is down time. All of us, as teachers, have made the mistake of saying, 'Okay, that completes today's lesson. You guys can talk quietly for the rest of the period.' But most young men don't know what 'quietly' means. As each minute goes by, the volume rises." We encourage our teachers to plan more activities than they think they will need, and to arrive with all their teaching materials already organized and ready to use, to make transitions between activities as seamless as they can. Leave a minute of idle time, and it may lead to a situation you have to clean up.

SUIT THEIR STYLE

Young men tend to have short attention spans. That's not true of all young men, and you will find some young women with short spans as well, but in a room full of young men you'll tend to have more kids with shorter attention spans than in a co-ed group. To suit them, we build in more transitions than you might find in a traditional class hour. Typically, a lesson begins with a problem or exercise to do right away (the "Do Now" I previously mentioned), then a mini lecture on new material, an activity to make that mini lecture practical, and a summary. With young men, it can be helpful to design in one or two more transitions. Similarly, many but not all young men enjoy technology, and can be encouraged to maintain focus when they get to use an engaging piece of technology. Many, too, are highly visual, and have an easier time grasping concepts and keeping focused when they can use their eyes and not just their ears. Highly structured lessons with lots of hands-on use of technology and lots of visual illustrations tend to hold our students' attention the longest.

REWARD SUCCESS

I've been talking so far about incentives and teaching methods that help young men get to work and stay at work. It's equally as important to let our young men know, from the beginning, that there will be rewards for actually completing the larger mission: doing excellent work and staying away from harmful situations. For kids who are really handling their business and doing the right thing, we offer a variety of rewards and new opportunities, such as internships, job leads, and opportunities to study abroad. Each year, we take a group of kids to the national conference of the 100 Black Men organization, whose New York City chapter founded Eagle Academy. That means a chance to travel to another city and stay in a hotel, which shows young people that the world is larger than they may have realized, and that there are practical traveling skills for getting around in it. We take a dozen of our most successful kids, in terms of both academics and character, to Disney World. We want to show our students that success on our terms, as opposed to the terms of the street, will bring them concrete benefits—the country and the entire world can open up to them. That's a motivation more powerful than any number of trips to the video-game room. And every year before the Disney World–bound group leaves, I've heard kids say, "Next year, Mr. Banks, it's going to be me in Disney World. I'm going to be there—you'll see!"

REAL WORLD PROBLEMS

The most successful month, educationally speaking, that I ever had began by chance. It was during my years at the Bronx School for Law, Government and Justice, during a lunch period, and I was standing with a student and looking out a classroom window. Across the street, workers were putting up a billboard, a cigarette advertisement.

"That's ridiculous!" I said to the student. "Don't they know there's a school right here? This is no place to be selling cigarettes."

The young man next to me said, "We should do something about that, Mr. Banks."

I brought his idea to the teachers, and they designed a school-wide unit around that billboard and the questions it raised. In science classes, students studied the harmful impact of nicotine on the body. In social studies, students researched the laws on tobacco, and discovered that there was already a law that limited advertising close to schools. However, at that time our school was inside an old factory building, so it was possible that there was some confusion. In math classes, students were doing a unit on estimation, so they worked on ways of estimating the distance from the front of the school to the billboard. In English classes they wrote letters to the mayor, the head of the city council, and local elected officials. Every class had a role in this unit that unfolded over the course of a month.

Soon, we got a phone call from the mayor's office. They said they appreciated all the information we sent and that the issue was going to be addressed. Then we learned that an extension of the law had been passed. The mayor was going to be signing it, and he invited our students to attend. We brought twenty-five kids to that bill signing at City Hall, and they stood side by side as he made it a law. At the press conference afterward, some of my students spoke about their experience. And within a week, we looked out our windows to see workers removing that billboard.

That to me is what education is all about. We started not just with some amorphous sense that it's good to study, but a clear mission: to become educated and active, so we can make our world a better place. Our students took their concepts and their practical skills, such as estimation and composition, and used what they were learning to get results they could see.

REMEDIATE TO ACCELERATE

Many of our students come to us below the level of academic achievement expected of college-bound scholars their age. On the first day of the big race to college, they are already behind. So how can they win a race when they haven't even reached the starting line? They have to speed up until they catch up, and then *keep putting on speed* until they make it to the front.

Some of our young men do come in with excellent skills, and find sixth grade easy. Their parents get concerned. We tell those parents, "Be patient. It's about to get a whole lot more challenging." What starts out looking like a remedial program transitions into a rigorous college-prep program simply by picking up the pace. New York City requires high schools to teach three years of math and science, but we want to do four years. We get our students up to grade level, then help them through the required courses sooner than the city requires so we have more time for advanced placement courses in the later years. We don't divide our students into the ones who need remedial work and the one who are "gifted." We remediate to accelerate.

SUPPORT THOSE WHO FALL BEHIND

If you urge young men to achieve more and faster, if you give them incentives and structure their time so they can accelerate their learning, inevitably some will stumble. Just as every race car driver needs a pit crew, and every marathoner needs water and food and moral support from assistants waiting along the route, at times our young men will need extra support along the way. At Eagle, we look for that support from the other communities that are invested in our young men's success—from their teachers, Eagle brothers, families at home, and mentors.

First, we rely on the teachers to come together regularly to discuss which students are falling behind in which classes and why that might be. In this common planning time, teachers can develop strategies to bring all the partners together. If a student is doing fine in most of his classes but struggling in one, it might be that the student needs to meet twice a week with the teacher of that class during the extended part of the school day. In addition to working with the student one on one, the teacher could look among the student's house brothers (see chapter three) to find a peer mentor who could work with him as well. Kids have their own ways of teaching one another, their own sense of what will make the struggling student say, "Oh! Is *that* what she meant?" And for the peer mentor, research shows, teaching someone else helps him take his own understanding of a subject to a further level—you have to get a lesson very clear in your own head if you're going to explain it to others. Soon the student who stumbled is back on his feet, and the student who tutored him is running faster than ever. They both advance.

What many of our students have to discover is that when they come up short, most of the time it's just a question of effort. It's not as though there's any serious hidden problem like a learning disability; it's just a matter of putting in the time to study. They will find that the kid sitting next to them who got a 94 isn't any smarter, he just studied more. During the week, in the afternoons, we provide an hour to an hour and a half of supervised study hall for those that need extra support in doing their homework. That eliminates the excuse of not having a quiet place at home. Over the weekends, we rely on parents to help make sure that homework and studying gets done.

Our teachers also work with parents to break the old habit of waiting for report cards and parent-teacher conferences to find out how their son is doing, and instead to follow their child's daily progress online. Grades and tests are posted every day, as are homework assignments. We remind our parents, "You can check our website from work if you like. You can see exactly the assignments he's getting, what he got on his quiz two days ago, what tests are coming up next. No surprises—it's all there!"

Often teachers find that the parents, like the students, need a few reminders of the higher level of engagement we expect before they get fully involved. The first time a teacher calls a parent to make sure the parent is encouraging serious study at home, the response may be something like, "Oh, well, I couldn't check online. I didn't get my password."

"Oh, you didn't get it?" the teachers will say. "Here it is again. Now, your son has another quiz coming up next week. Let's see how he does then." It's another area in which the teachers may have to teach the parents to support the students.

We look to our teachers to use their common planning time to share what they've come to know about the families. Sometimes it isn't helpful to call a student's parents, because the student is being raised primarily by another family member. A teacher who knows the student's family story can share that kind of information with the student's other teachers—*I'll give you the cell number for his grandma. She's the one he listens to.*

We want our students to feel that when they have difficulty in school, they can run but they can't hide. Just as I learned when my father would stop by school unexpectedly, we want all our students to know that at any moment, someone may be watching them—and looking out for them. If they do well, we will acknowledge and reward them. If they are struggling, we will help them find support. The entire Eagle family isn't going to let them fail. The child or children you're responsible for must feel the same.

A COACH FOR THE WHOLE TEAM

I have said that the job of teachers is not simply teaching subjects such as social studies or algebra, it is teaching young people with all their particular needs. At Eagle, our job is teaching young men, and we must look for those who understand that mission. In the same way, a school needs a leader who understands that the job involves not just fulfilling the educational requirements of being a principal, but fulfilling the needs of the school in its neighborhood with its particular population. It is as much a community leadership and communications role as it is an educational role.

Think of basketball. Five players play their different positions. If you look at a diagram of those positions—guards, center, and forwards—and a list of their responsibilities in the game, basketball can sound pretty simple. What makes the game complex is that the players don't stand still. Every player is in motion most of the time, and must communicate with and support the others as they play. It's so complex that the best teams all have a group of coaches off the court, observing, planning, advising, and trying to keep everyone playing their best together.

In the same way, a school can sound simple when you consider the parts in isolation: students, teachers, administrators, parents, and so forth. But all of these parts must be in motion at the same time—and the whole project only succeeds when someone is making sure that each of the players works to support the others, so that all the needs are met. A basketball coach observes and coordinates his or her players; in a roughly similar way, the principal and the other members of the Eagle school leadership must observe, coordinate, and motivate the entire "team."

GIVE TEACHERS TIME TO REFLECT AND CHANGE

These forms of support depend on teachers talking to one another while there is still time to make changes in their approach. We need teachers to raise red flags about students when they've been going wrong for just a week or two, not when they're on the list to receive failing grades. We need teachers talking with their principal and assistant principal about what they are *planning* to teach, not just being evaluated for the units they have already taught. At Eagle, while our students are eating lunch, we build in a common planning period. This is a chance for teachers to talk about individual students, to coordinate interdisciplinary units like that response to the tobacco billboard, and to reflect overall on the results they are getting in the classrooms and the alternatives they could try.

We need teachers who want to be part of a learning organization. We don't have one perfect method for teaching young men, and we never will. But what lets us continue to improve is that we continue to get to know our young men, to observe their progress, and to reflect on the choices we've made to support their education, which in turn lets us continue to suit our method to their changing needs.

CHAPTER FIVE

A CONSPIRACY OF CARE

The Power of Love, Security, and High Expectations

Why did we lose Edward? I can still picture him in our first-ever freshman class, a handsome fourteen-year-old with curly hair and big dark eyes, wearing an expensive leather jacket. This was during Eagle Academy's first year as a school, and though we were a school for boys, we shared a building with a larger co-ed school. The girls noticed Edward and talked to him in the hall. Edward smiled a lot, but it was a cunning smile, a smile you weren't sure you could trust, revealing the buck teeth of a teenager who still sucked his thumb at night.

Teachers complained that Edward Gordon was disruptive. Some of the students said he was funny. But there have been plenty of disruptive students whom we have turned around—often the disruptive ones reveal themselves to be natural leaders who haven't yet directed their leadership skills in productive ways. Even so, we lost

Edward. He left the school after one year and broke ties with everyone there. Last I heard he was in prison for a violent crime.

One reason we couldn't get through to Edward was a simple lack of time. He left us after only a year. Another reason: the school was still new, and we hadn't fully developed all of the elements of the Eagle method. The house system I described in chapter three was not yet in place, and I don't think he ever felt the positive peer pressure of the Eagle brotherhood.

I wish I could say that at least one member of our staff got a glimpse beneath his armor and saw a chance for him to break out, but none of us did. What we knew was that Edward felt a different kind of peer pressure. He had an older brother he idolized, someone he talked about when he was in school. This brother looked out for him, Edward said. He even bought Edward leather 8-Ball jackets in different colors. He could afford them because he was a drug dealer bringing in good money.

That older brother, more than anything, was the obstacle to our work. Aaron Barnette, our dean of students in the Bronx, explains, "It's one thing to have a tug of war for a kid between Eagle and the streets. But when the tug on the other side is coming from home, that makes it much tougher." When we tried to talk to Edward about his future, about what he could make of his life if he changed the ways he spent his time and the people he spent it with, he wasn't interested. He didn't need to change the people he spent his time with because he felt good about those he had. He didn't need to prepare for a career—why did he need a career? A degree? He was going to be dealer like his brother. When we matched him up with a mentor, he wasn't impressed. He had a mentor already. And his mentor wasn't just a father figure, he was real family.

THE POWER OF FAMILY

Losing Edward, first to the streets and then to the criminal justice system, was a cruel reminder of just how powerful a family's influence can be, for better or worse. Students spend the greatest part of their time, besides the hours they are in school, with their families. As educational researcher J. S. Coleman first demonstrated in the 1960s, student success depends not just on what happens in school, but on the learning that goes on at home. The elements of what Coleman termed "comprehensive education" include everything from mealtime conversations and family trips to observing parents solving problems and doing their jobs. The example and the encouragement students get at home, whether for good or for bad, can make all the difference in whether a school can get through to them.

It's easiest to see the tremendous power of families, traditional or otherwise, in the stories of those young men who received little positive family influence. Kalim Jones was another of our students that first year in the Bronx. He'd never met his father. He was raised by his mother, but she had a drug addiction. As Kalim describes it: "When she was on the drug, her personality flipped. She would be so distant, cold—a vacant soul. She was there physically in the apartment or the homeless shelter, but she wasn't there to support me. If I needed her to come to a parent-teacher conference, she would tell me, 'I'm busy that day,' which was strange because I knew she didn't have a job.

"When I brought my grades home, she'd look at my report card and say, 'Okay, good.' It didn't matter what the numbers were. I brought home eighties, seventies, knowing I could do much better. She said, 'Okay, good.'" At times, Kalim ran away to stay with relatives "to feel that I belonged somewhere," but he always came home again, in part because he had two younger siblings and felt that he had to look out for them.

In ninth grade, when he came to Eagle, Kalim made a name for himself with his full-throated screaming arguments with teachers and staff, especially the men. He had fistfights with other students. He had a noisy way of sucking his teeth—in the middle of class, or when an adult was trying to speak to him—that could get under your skin.

In tenth grade, one morning a teacher reminded him to take off his sweater because it wasn't part of his school uniform. As Kalim tells the story, on that morning he wasn't cold, but he felt so enraged at being told what to do that he began shouting and things escalated. He wound up being suspended for five days for insubordination and disrespecting a faculty member.

Defiant and rebellious, Kalim was almost incapable of trust. He seemed to believe that most adults, especially the males, were out to do him harm. He remembers being the kind of kid who made adults say, "You're never going to amount to anything." In response, he would laugh, as if it were all a joke to him. I remember warning him that with his attitude it didn't seem like he was going to be at Eagle very long.

PARENTS: NOT WORTH THE RISK?

Dr. Howard Fuller, educational reformer, describes what he calls his "politically incorrect guide" to family influence. He sees four possible categories of family members, which includes older siblings, aunts and grandparents, legal guardians, foster parents—everyone who has a sustained influence on a young man by their presence or their absence:

1. Those telling kids the right thing to do, contributing to their education, and getting through to them.
2. Those telling kids the right thing, but not in a way the kids can feel it. These parents come to teachers and administrators desperate for help.
3. Those who don't care about school. They don't make themselves available to teachers. They don't necessarily provide the school with accurate phone numbers for reaching them. Their attitude seems to be that if a teacher or school administrator contacts them, it's a waste of the parent's time.

4. Those who are actively hostile toward school and its goals. Some examples include the parent who curses out a child for being so full of himself that he thinks he's going to college or the parent who knows that the child's school has a zero-tolerance policy for drugs, but gets high with the child anyway.

Out of Fuller's four categories, only one is successful, and that may be a clue to why so many schools seem to treat their students' families as a danger to be minimized. Not just in urban schools but across the country, the larger educational system does not generally try to engage parents as educational partners. In the case of boarding schools, of course, parents are generally far away, with little influence over students' day-to-day education. And at some charter schools, the attitude is: *You bring your child to us, and we'll take it from there.*

Even schools that hang out banners that read WELCOME PARENTS often don't, in fact, welcome them. Many school administrators whom I speak to privately make it clear that they are unsure how to engage parents and, more than that, they doubt that parent engagement is a good idea. They don't believe parents and other family can understand what the school is trying to do. They worry that having family members in school means there would be prying eyes and ears ready to stir up trouble and make the administrators' lives more difficult. It makes some administrators feel, frankly, insecure. And so the real message to families may well be: *Parents, you make sure the kids get to bed on time and that they get to school in the morning. After that, we'll call you if we need you.* They may want parents to make financial and other kinds of practical contributions, but the overall educational goal is to keep parents at a distance and minimize the harm they can do.

That's not the approach we take at Eagle. We have found that we can't succeed without our community of parents, because parents have a double influence on the success of their young men: first, in the direct ways in which they either support or weaken their sons' efforts at home, and second, in the ways they strengthen the school, so the institution is better able to take care of their boys. We have come to believe that our best chance of giving our students the comprehensive education they need, and their best chance of succeeding, is if the school helps families to support their children's education as fully as they can—and to reinforce those efforts when they fall short.

We have to be prepared for those new Eagle parents who are not so different from our new students: unprepared, at first, for what Eagle asks of them, but capable of learning, excelling, and making better lives for themselves and their families. We must help our families to become the sort that can help our students to excel as scholars and as citizens.

REBUILDING TRUST

If we had gotten more of a chance to work with Edward, whose mentor brother was teaching him skills that would lead him, if not to prison, than certainly nowhere inspiring, we might have been able to help him build more productive relationships with other teachers and mentors. But could we "reinforce" the family relationships of a student whose circumstances were as challenging as Kalim's? With a history like his, was there enough family support to give even the most well-meaning educators something to work with?

Had you been one of the adults—men especially—that he screamed at and fought with, you might have doubted whether anyone could get through to a kid betrayed so badly for so long by both of his parents. And yet Kalim still hungered for love and good parenting, and tried to make his way toward a better life.

When he was twelve, before he came to Eagle, Kalim met a girl his age who became a friend. Sometimes she would invite him to her house. Alone together, they would talk and watch movies, and he would escape from his home life for a few hours. One day she asked him to meet her at her church. When the day came, Kalim remembered the street name, but not the name of the church. He found that there were four churches on the block, and though he looked among the pews at all four, he couldn't find his young friend.

Kalim was usually very shy, but that day he walked up to a Caribbean lady dressed for church and asked if she knew his friend. She told him she didn't, but offered that Kalim could come in, sit beside her, and listen to the word of God. The sermon was on meeting the difficult challenges of life, and as the minister spoke, Kalim wept. Afterward, the woman asked him if his mother would permit her to bring him home and make him lunch.

He told her, "She wouldn't care either way."

That was the beginning of a lasting relationship. The woman he called Miss Tiddle would invite him to her home, talk with him about his life, feed him when he was hungry, buy him clothes, and teach him some of the things his mother was too distracted to explain. She showed him how to eat politely, and what fork, knife, and spoon to use for different dishes. She explained basic etiquette and grooming, and the importance of looking presentable and speaking well. She made him feel there was someone watching out for him, someone he didn't want to disappoint.

By the time Kalim came to Eagle Academy, Miss Tiddle had died in a car accident, and he had no one to talk with the way he used to talk with her. Soon he was drifting, fighting with students and staff, and he often found himself in detention. There, like all the Eagles in detention that day, he would get a visit from Yvette Crespo, who was then the family coordinator. She let him tell her how he had wound up in detention that day. Ms. Crespo showed an interest in his feelings, but as Kalim remembers, "At first, I didn't believe her. I didn't believe anybody."

Ms. Crespo began to talk to him about her own childhood. Her relationship with her own mother had been very difficult, and she had joined a gang. "I only opened up to her," Kalim says, "because she shared some of her personal stories with me, about how she grew up, the challenges she faced with her own mother, who was very hard on her."

Slowly, he came to accept Ms. Crespo's offer that he could come by her office when he needed to talk. She gave him her personal cell phone number and he memorized it. She began to speak to him about his potential, reminding him often that he could do something great with his life if he believed in himself.

Kalim began to participate in every after-school program, school trip, and Eagle open house that he could. He often stayed at school in the evenings with a small group of students who had nowhere else to go, doing homework and helping out Ms. Crespo in small ways, sometimes until seven at night. Other kids asked him, "Why are you always here?" He had found his adoptive home.

By the eleventh grade, although his mother was still moving the family among homeless shelters, Kalim was talking out his feelings more than acting them out. His behavior improved, as did his grades. When he met with Donald Ruff, the college counselor, his first reaction was distrust, but Ms. Crespo was there to vouch for Ruff, and to remind Kalim of what was now a significant history of adults, female and male, who had believed in him and won his trust, building on what Miss Tiddle had started: Ms. Crespo, teachers, counselors, administrators, and others in the Eagle family who acted in many ways as surrogate parents. In time, Kalim allowed Ruff to guide him through the long college application process. Writing his application essay, Kalim told his personal story in detail for the first time. He was starting to show what he could do.

BLACK-AND-WHITE MOVIES

Security, high expectations, and love are basic needs for all children, but parents and other caring adults can provide them—and children can find them—in a lot of ways. By *security*, I don't mean just the physical protection of safe passage through the neighborhood, but the emotional safety that comes when a child understands: *For now, you can just be a child. You don't have to take on the adult roles of protector or provider. You don't have to be the mama or daddy bear just yet.* In my own childhood, I remember having that feeling most clearly when the family watched old movies together. For years, my dad would say to my brothers and me, "Who wants to watch a black-and-white movie?" He meant that we should watch some old classic together, like *Cyrano de Bergerac,* the 1950 film about the great sword fighter and poet Cyrano, who is too self-conscious about his big nose to woo the beautiful and intelligent heiress, Roxane.

Some of these movies were inspiring and full of valuable lessons. Some were pretty corny, and at times we complained, but underneath we loved it all. The truth is that kids hunger for the corny stuff, because if they feel safe enough with their families to watch some corny old movie, it shows that they must really be children, and it's still all right for them to be mothered, daddied, and enclosed in the protective stronghold of their parents. Watching those old movies, I think my brothers and I all felt: *Here we are, encircled by love.*

I made a point of creating those moments for my own kids as well. We would climb onto the bed and watch old black-and-white classics or Disney movies, all of us together, with the kids in their pajamas, sharing a big bowl of popcorn. My wife and I might be under the covers, my son Ali lying over there under a blanket sucking his thumb, Rashaad by his knee, my daughter, Aaliyah, at the foot of the bed, and Jamal lying against his mother's knee. I remember those moments when I would look up and think, *I love this. It doesn't get any better than this. This is what family is supposed to be.* A little later I might look around and see that someone had fallen asleep, and that was fine. The whole point was that we all felt so comfortable and so safe, one could just drift off, because we were all there together.

During moments like that, young men find the sanctity of love and security. I name the two separately because you need both. The experience is completely different if you have one without the other—either love combined with fear, like what those who are abused may experience, or cold, loveless safety, like that felt by a prisoner in a cell. Kids need love and security together and they need them above everything else. Their spirits are yearning for them, no matter what comes out of their mouths.

For different families, they come in different ways. Some may find love and security while singing together. Some may find them while baking together, when even the big kids want to help measure and mix, and to lick the bowl and the spoon. Some may find them during that sleepy time on a weekend morning, when everyone gathers together in one bedroom. When my daughter was grown, I took her to an old-school concert at Jones Beach featuring the O'Jays, the Spinners, and so many other groups she'd heard growing up. My groups. I wanted her to spend that evening with me. There weren't a lot of young people there, it was an older crowd, but she had a blast watching some of the older folks dancing in the aisles. She loved being a part of it even though her friends wouldn't find it new or cool—in fact, exactly because it wasn't.

I know Kalim found something like that with the other kids who stayed into the evening in Ms. Crespo's office, just hanging around together long after their homework was done, glad not to have to leave quite yet, even as it grew dark. That was his place to belong, his place to feel sheltered.

Nothing is more meaningful to a child, and nothing is needed more urgently, than to feel loved, to feel safe, and to feel that the person who keeps him loved and safe has high expectations for him. Of course, a teenage boy may not tell you that directly—he may not seem to acknowledge it at all. But it's no less true, even if the feelings may be too intense and intimate to talk about.

MAMA BEAR LOVE

I have stories I like to share with our students and their parents to illustrate what we hope for our young men to find both in school and at home. The first story comes from a vacation that I took with my family in the Poconos. We were outside in front of the little cabin we had rented in the mountains, enjoying the day, when one of my kids called out, "Oh, look! They're so cute!" Three tiny black bear cubs were walking right by our cabin. At first we were all completely charmed—those roly-poly little cubs were adorable—but then it hit me.

"Wait a minute!" I called out, "If there are Cubs, then there's a mama bear nearby. Everybody back inside! We'll watch from there."

I opened the door and my wife and I got the kids back into the cabin as fast as we could. Within seconds, this big mama bear came following the cubs. I remember thinking, *Holy smokes!* If we had tried to touch or approach those cute little cubs, she would have seen us as a threat, and a mama bear will fight you to the death to protect her cubs.

As we observed, we saw that she wasn't just ready to fight. She was equally ready to care for her children, to pick them up, to lick them, to nurse them, and to play with them. You could see in those few moments how well those cubs were loved and protected. When we got back home I told the story several times, and someone said to me, "If only all our parents were like that. If only all of them felt, *My whole life depends on taking care of these babies.*"

I have to add that educators can be too quick to talk about the families in extreme situations—the father in jail, the mother on drugs, the kids left to fend for themselves. Those stories catch everyone's attention and remind us all just how much is at stake when parents fall apart, but they are not the stories of typical parents. Most parents don't fall apart. Even in the "prison pipeline" neighborhoods where we build Eagle schools, most parents are hardworking, well-meaning people with a lot of responsibilities, a lot of different demands they have to meet. They are people who would appreciate some help and guidance when their young men start acting a little wild and need to be given greater structure and a clearer sense of what's expected. So I want to offer some guidance now for what I think those expectations should be, and then for what parents can do when their young men are not living up to them.

HIGH EXPECTATIONS

It might seem as if nothing could be less like the warm, comforting protection I'm describing than high expectations of achievement, but what is it to love someone if not to want the best for that person? What does it mean to care for a young man if not to want him to realize his gifts, be true to himself, and make a good life in which he can provide love and security for others? To do those things, to take risks, to fall down and get back up, he will need confidence and a secure sense of himself, and for that he will draw on his memories of being loved and held safe.

The key is to provide our children with these seeming opposites all at once. Kalim not only missed out on caring and safety, he also had no one to say to him, "You have been given gifts. You can get higher grades, you can follow these rules, and you can make your school and your parents proud. The sky's the limit."

TAKE CARE OF YOUR BUSINESS FIRST

My parents' expectations for my brothers and me were expressed through a very simple rule we often heard growing up. A lot of parents let the kids rip and run after school, and in the little bit of time left over, with the little bit of energy that remains, the students get to their schoolwork. But our father said, "Your homework gets done *first.*" It wasn't just a rule about homework; it was a lesson in getting the priorities straight: when you're young it's your business to be a student, and when you're in school, you have to handle your business. Do your homework. Follow the rules. Be respectful to your teachers. *You do your work first, and then there will be time to play and to relax.*

In the same way, a parent needs to put his or her foot down so kids can rest. They can't hang out until all hours of the night. I can remember my father taking a very hard line with me about this. "If I tell you to be back by eight o'clock, that doesn't mean eight-thirty and it doesn't mean eight-fifteen." Once the kids are home, there needs to be a clear bedtime when all the screens are off (phones, too) so they can get a good night's sleep and be ready for the next day. I often tell my students, "It's impossible to hoot with the owls at night and soar with the eagles at dawn."

SOMEONE IS WATCHING

As a boy, when I was in class, I would look up sometimes and see my father's face at the door, framed in that little classroom window. He would come to school in his police uniform. Sometimes I didn't see him right away, and another kid would whisper, "Your dad's at the door, Dave." I would just keep doing my work.

It's one thing if a son knows a parent is coming in on Tuesday at 9:00 a.m. to meet with one certain teacher. That's just one hour out of hundreds. It's a different deal if a parent might show up at any time, unannounced. That keeps a child minding his p's and q's. In my family, my mom and dad had it set up well. My mom's schedule was more routine; we knew when she was getting home and we relied on her—but we also knew that if we wanted to get into mischief, we were okay as long as we got done before she came home. Our dad, though, was very hard to track. He would slip in from any angle. It seemed like he was everywhere. You could run but you couldn't hide.

I believe our goal as parents is to give children a sense not just of love and protection, but of a watchful presence that knows what they're up to and expects it to be something good. (At Eagle, parents are permitted to show up at school to check on their children, but also strongly encouraged to contact the administration of the school beforehand, so they can arrange to appear when the student is in a class where he might need extra supervision. Not a lot of parents do this, but when they do, word gets around among the students and at the parents' meetings.) The practical benefits come both in terms of holding students to a higher standard and also in showing love. When parents come to school, and when it feels like they might do so again soon, it intensifies the feeling that I believe any child may get when parents appear: *They're here? This must matter. I must matter. They cared enough to come today.*

YOU NEVER KNOW WHO IS WATCHING

We want our Eagle parents to provide the sense that they're watching for their own children, but also to help provide that sense for the whole Eagle community. Kenyatte Reid, principal of Eagle Academy in Queens, likes to share a story about a phone call he received from a parent who had stopped by the school and then, on her way out, saw a student making some trouble out on the street. She called the principal and said, "Mr. Reid, you have a young man outside who's not acting right." Mr. Reid walked out of the building and confronted the young man, who looked all around, in every direction, confused. Finally he asked, "Mr. Reid, who told you?"

"You never know who's watching," Mr. Reid replied.

An experience like that could stay with that young man for a long time. It's a model we offer all of our parents: keep your eye out not just for your own kids, but for other Eagle students and other students in your neighborhood. Know your child's friends, and make sure you meet their parents. If you have a concern, call them up. If your son doesn't understand an assignment, if your son is having a problem that another child could help with, even if he has an early game tomorrow and he'd get more sleep if he stayed with someone who lives closer to the school—make the call. Keep an eye out for the way our young men are behaving and for the ways we could help them to succeed. That's part of being a committed parent. I had that kind of community growing up, but any group of committed parents can build this type of community, or rebuild it where it has been lost.

When you listen to children talk about adults, they sometimes make it sound as if there are two kinds, the "nice," loving ones and the "mean" ones who impose rules. But what we need our parents to understand is that the rules, as serious as they may be, should grow out of love and show our young people that they are loved.

I want to share more of the rules I grew up with, rules that are also part of our approach at Eagle, and that, of course, you can implement, too. Each rule has practical value, establishing the high expectations we have for our young men, but all of them come from a place of love.

COMMON TIME

When I was growing up, we all wanted our own televisions. That was the dream: to have your own room with your own television so you didn't have to come out into the living room and deal with others in the family who might want to watch something else. Now children want not just televisions but also computers, video-game systems, smartphones, tablets, and who knows what will come next. They want all their devices all the time and they don't want to share. But as my dad used to say, "If you had everything in your room, what reason would you have to come out and talk with us?"

In our house, there was only one television, and because there was only one, we all had to negotiate together about what we were going to see. We might not always have gotten to watch our first choice, but we were together and we were talking about it. That shared time—talking in the living room, talking around the dinner table—is essential, but it's ever more endangered. That's the time when kids learn how adults talk to one another. That's when they benefit from the "comprehensive education" that goes beyond anything that can happen in the classroom. That's when they learn the basic social skills that help people get along even when they're under pressure—the stuff you don't miss until people around you stop doing it, such as asking, "How was your day? What did you learn today?" The most important topics often come up unscripted, just because there's time in the day or the week to let a strong feeling or a nagging question come up. But if it's going to happen, I believe parents have to make a conscious choice to arrange the home and the week so that there is time and space for family talk.

Sometimes the only way to get young men to talk is not to allow them to disappear into a screen. You have to set time aside, put away the electronics (which means parents have to do the same), and tolerate the complaining that's likely to come before the real conversation gets going. Dinner together with the whole family is the gold standard, but I know a family who can't be together for dinner on weeknights, so they make a rule that on Saturday, before everybody takes off, the whole family has breakfast together.

As kids get older, especially in the teenage years, it helps to have formal family meetings. I liked to call meetings once a week, if possible, and ask, What's going on in our home? What's going well? What needs to change? This was a good time for me to tell my kids which tasks and challenges I had seen them handle especially well. A chance to tell them, "I'm very proud of you—very, very proud of you. You did such a good job. I loved the way you handled it." I always took care to focus on the positive.

My own family benefitted most when there was a lot of open communication, a lot of time for talks with the kids—talking one-on-one, talking in groups, planned meetings, and spontaneous conversations. I was not running a dictatorship, more of a directed democracy. If there was no talk, then either the kids were running wild, missing out on all that their parents could teach them, or the rules and decisions came down to the parents saying, "You do what I say, period." That stance is very dangerous for young people. If we fail to teach our kids *why* some choices are better than others, they won't have the understanding to apply those rules when the parents aren't there to tell them exactly what to do, or when life comes at them a little differently than what we described for them.

Will you get some resistance? Sure. Sometimes my kids would drag themselves in as if it was the last thing they wanted to do—"Oh, no! Family meeting. Not again!" But I noticed something. If a week or two went by and we didn't get around to it, my kids would ask me, "Dad? Aren't we supposed to be doing the family meeting?"

It turned out that my kids loved those meetings. They discovered that this was the time to share their thoughts and feelings and have the rest of us pay attention. For me, that was the best part of it: to get to hear them speak their own minds and their own hearts. Sometimes we would sit for quite a while sharing our opinions, getting to know what was new in one another's lives, and taking pleasure in this great gift of family, even forgetting our electronics. That helped me realize: you can't allow yourself to be dissuaded from insisting on common time just because kids mope and groan. Stay the course! They may be angry for a while when you tell them no—no television in your room, not even if you earn the money yourself; no, you can't check your texts during family meetings—but they will be glad later for what you preserved for them by saying no.

NOTHING GIVEN, EVERYTHING EARNED

When I first became a school principal, I had a student, a ninth grader, fourteen years old, and already a mother. Exceptionally bright, she had experienced far too much of life for her fourteen years. I remember she liked to show me when she had a big pocketful of cash. She would pull out a hundred or two hundred dollars, just to show me what she was carrying. One day she asked me, "Mr. Banks, how much money do you give *your* kids?"

"I don't give my kids money," I said.

"That doesn't make sense!" she said. "You have a good job. Can't you afford to give your kids any money?"

"My kids don't need a pocketful of cash," I told her. "They already have breakfast, lunch, and dinner, and if there's something I agree they should buy then I will give them money for it."

I understand how badly parents want to give their children what they themselves didn't have growing up. That's the reason I'll find parents who I know are struggling to make ends meet standing on line outside the shoe store because the latest sneakers just came out for two hundred dollars and they feel their nine-year-old has got to have them. That's the reason parents who have had financial success as adults will shower their kids with material things: the latest phone, the latest computer, and a television in every room. But that's not helping our young people. That's stealing from them.

At Eagle we say, "Everything is earned, nothing is given." That's a financial lesson, but the core comes from love and nurturance. I've seen so many kids who get money from their parents to make them feel better when something is wrong, or because the parents had very little growing up and they vowed to give their kids more. But so often the parents overcompensate, and wind up giving things to kids so early and so suddenly that the kids don't appreciate what they're given.

When kids have to wait until they earn something—whether it's money they made at a job or the privilege of being on the basketball team because they kept their grades up—they feel the value of it. That's what helps kids to understand and appreciate the many blessings they have in life. A little sacrifice breeds character. When you eliminate all the waiting and working from a child's life, and make it possible for them to have whatever they want at the moment it first occurs to them, you are not helping them. You are emptying their lives of meaning.

What do kids need, if not a wad of cash in their pocket? They need parents to bring them along with them, talk to them, and stay close to them. When I used to leave the house to do an errand, I'd always try to bring one of my kids with me. I'd grab one of my kids and say, "Come on, let's walk to the store—we'll be back in twenty minutes." It was another chance to show them the spirit of love that says, *It's not the things.* You *are what's most important to me, and I love you.*

A FEW GOOD MEN

Some children are blessed with dedicated, involved fathers in their lives. But for those who are not, it is critically important to find a few reliable, employed, responsible men—whether an uncle, a grandfather, a neighbor, or someone from church—to be part of their lives. To serve as guideposts as they navigate the journey toward adulthood. Young men and young women need good models of manhood. And if the kids are acting up, if they are not respecting the mother who cares for them or the rules of the house, then Mom can call on one of the men in that child's life to come have a conversation. *What's going on with you? Why are you not listening to your mother, your grandmother, your aunt? Why are you not paying attention?* The point of these conversations may be to admonish, but also to listen, to let the child be heard and to discover again that he is cared for. Sometimes just having a caring figure, not the primary parent, who will listen to a young person's frustrations about the rules will make it easier for the child to do the right thing. That's a part of mentoring, which I'll have more to say about in the next chapter.

ENGAGE THE PARENTS

Rules like the ones I've just described will have the most impact on our young men if they are applied consistently at home and at school. But educators have a lot more control of the school environment than of the homes our students return to when they leave us. Principals can pick their teachers. They can put rules in place to help nurture brotherhood among the students, and discipline or even expel those who don't follow the rules. They can tell students outright, "It's your parents' job to ask what you're learning, how your work is coming, and whether you are building good relationships with your teachers. It's part of their job to help you to become scholars, gentlemen, and productive members of the community. You may not always like it, but that's what parents are supposed to do." But no school official can fire a bad parent or hire better ones. We can't send parents to remedial classes if they flunk Intro to Fatherhood and Motherhood. We want them to serve as our co-teachers and co-administrators, but how do we influence the parents to support our work when we have no formal control of them at all?

Most schools have a wish list of help they want from their parents. Communication between administration and parents is a simple transaction: the school asks for what it needs, some parents respond but many don't, and then both go on separately until the school asks for more. Parent participation tends not to be that high and the school community may not feel like a community at all.

At Eagle, instead of that two-step transaction—school asks, parents give or slink away—we try to make the conversation last a little longer. To begin, we don't ask the parents for anything. We try to show them, instead, that they are welcome at their son's school, and that it's worth their while to come to our events and meetings because of what we can offer them. We are trying to show them what's in it for them when they join the sort of community that will benefit their children.

What do parents need? My wife and I raised four children, and along with the joy of it, I will never forget how challenging it could be. Parents get *tired*. I remember so well coming home to four small kids. Every evening, I intended to, at the very least, pick each child up and read each one of them a book. But sometimes I would come through that front door so ready to lie down myself, and I would feel, *Well, maybe not today.*

Anyone who accepts even part-time responsibility for a young person winds up taxed in ways he or she didn't anticipate, in situations he or she is not prepared for, with more questions than answers. Children come with no owner's manual and are fully explained by no Wiki-parenting website. There is really no app for any of it. Some parents are living the American dream, owning their own home, with Mom and Dad gainfully employed like my parents back on our block in Queens, but even so, raising a family is a challenge. If we're honest, all of us who share responsibility for how a young man turns out will find ourselves wondering at times: How are we going to keep this up? Wondering if we are one hundred percent certain of the decisions we had to make as parents last month. You'll find most people at least partly making it up as they go along. Everyone could use some help.

From the first days that we meet prospective Eagle families at our open houses, we try to show not just the students but the parents what our Eagle community has to offer. We bring existing Eagle students and Eagle parents to talk to our prospective families about what excites them, from the mentoring program to our after-school activities such as sports, robotics, chess, and culinary arts. Those first presentations give young men something to connect to, and even a glimmer of a connection can awaken the wishes in their parents' hearts: *I want my son to feel excited about school. I don't want a fight just to get him out of bed. I want him to wake up eager for his day. I want to see him excited to learn.*

Then, at our End of the Year ceremony, when our new students come together for the first time before the Summer Bridge program, we begin to show our families what we expect of them as Eagles. The ceremony is as much for the new parents as it is for the new students. The principal chooses a guest speaker, and in the past I have asked Reverend Jacques DeGraff, a member of One Hundred Black Men and one of the founders of Eagle Academy. After the rising freshman walked in together, welcomed by a standing ovation, Reverend De-Graff stood tall at the podium, his hair showing silver at the temples, and spoke from long experience about the dangers facing our young men in the inner city.

"The criminal justice system has taken so many. But these you cannot have! These young men are meant for something different!"

The new parents were rapt. They understood better than their sons the odds these young men were up against. All over the gym, there were parents nodding. There were parents in tears. These were parents feeling that they needed help if their young men were going to beat the odds. These were parents daring to hope that we could help them.

At the same time, throughout this meeting and at every Eagle event, members of the administration and staff, as well as parents of older Eagle students, were there to welcome them. We hire administrators who respect parents. I have invited parent representatives to every meeting that effects the establishment and the future of an Eagle school—if there's a meeting with a school board, a mayor, a governor, I want parents there with me. I don't see them as my customers, buying my educational product as an investment in their sons' future. They're part of my family, a family that exists to help these young men to flourish and to succeed. I want to awaken that shared sense of a loving mission—because that mission can motivate a community to give their all.

At the conclusion of the End of the Year ceremony, we like to have all the men in the audience form a circle around the auditorium. They hold hands to close the circle with the women and children inside. One man leads a pledge that the rest repeat. "Herein lies the essence of our community, our women and our children. We as men assert that we will protect them. We will be real men, responsible men, supporting our mothers and wives, our daughters and sons."

When that is over, so many of the new parents—whether it's the fathers who have had the chance to make that circle of love and protection or the mothers who were held inside it—feel that this school is not like other schools they have known. It has a powerful aura, a mystique. It promises to be that rare place where deep emotional needs can be met, a place of security and love.

I say straight out to our parents, "Send us your children and we will cherish them as you cherish them at home. Your child will be my child!" There is power in that. So many parents feel, "If you want me to respond, be good to my child." When we show our love for our young men, not only can we win them over, we can win the parents, too.

Mr. Barnette, our dean of students, once put it this way at a Senior Convocation. "These are my little brothers. It takes a lot of energy to stay on top of these guys. Understand that we love you! Understand that we love you! Understand that we love you!" Not once, but three times, to let them know that love is the basis of male relationships, the basis and moving force of Eagle Academy.

That's the opposite of what many of our families expect. Principal Kenyatte Reid was a middle school principal before he came to Eagle. His middle school graduates used to come back and tell him, "I learned the difference between middle school and high school, Mr. Reid. In high school, they barely know my name. In high school, no one cares."

From our first day with new families we set out to prove those expectations wrong. Eagle families discover our love for our young men, and that feeling comes not just from the dean of students or the principal, not just from the director of admissions or the college coordinator, but from so many teachers and other staff. The more our parents get to know the school, the more they will find good-intentioned people, passionate about their sons. Many of our parents tell us that at the End of the Year ceremony, they felt right away, *This place is the place we have been hoping for. If this school can protect and love and motivate my son, then I have to get involved.*

It is then, after we have made our promise to help parents provide their boys with security, high expectations, and love, that we communicate another, complementary message. We explain that not just the young men but also the parents have obligations that come along with the opportunities. We tell the families, "You are not going to drop your sons off and come back to pick them up four years later. That's not happening here!"

For a parent dealing with a child, it's necessary sometimes to make clear that certain responsibilities are not negotiable. (One of our students explained the difference family made in his education this way. "I haven't missed one day of school—my mom doesn't allow it!") We've found that our parents need to hear a similarly strong, insistent voice, too. "We've got high expectations for your sons, and we have some high expectations for you." We explain that just as we expect our students to accept our challenge and learn what we teach, we expect our parents to learn what it takes to "raise a scholar."

We understand that "family" and "parent" mean different things for different students. Some of our students have two parents at home; a few, like Charles Miller, only the father; and many, like Kalim Jones, only the mother. Some are being raised by a grandmother or an auntie. Some, like Edward Gordon, may look primarily to an older brother or an uncle to show them how to live. But we tell every Eagle family, "You must participate in this school and in this child's education. We need every family encouraging and supervising their child's academic commitments at home; we need every family represented at our parent meetings and convocations; we're counting on all of you to volunteer somehow in the school. If no one in the immediate family can be here to support your child on a given day, send a relative, a next-door neighbor, a best friend—but make sure someone shows up as family for your young man."

That might sound like the end of the process of engaging families—first, we inspire them by promising help with the complex task of raising their sons, and then we ask them to participate. In fact, that is only the beginning of getting to know our students and their families, their needs and how we can help to meet them. One way we do that is to give families different ways to tell us about themselves. Yvette Crespo, who became director of admissions in the Bronx, meets one-on-one with each new Eagle family. The agenda is simple. She says, "Tell me about you," and she listens. The goal is to understand each student's individual situation well enough so that teachers and administrators can actively help each family. After the family session, we can begin to suggest connections with faculty and others in the Eagle community who can help their son to succeed.

From the start of these relationships with Eagle parents, we want to show them that being in contact with the school administration doesn't mean that their child is doing something wrong. Just as we look for opportunities to praise our young men, we look for chances to praise our parents for their efforts and for their sons' successes. Even a problem with a student can create the opportunity for a positive conversation. If a student is having an issue with attendance, we don't want the family to believe that we will only call when the young man has cut school. When the student comes to school, we might ask him to call home and let a family member know that all's well—"I'm in school today." We give the parent an opportunity to praise the child, and to feel good about a phone call from school.

DIRECT HELP FOR PARENTS

From 6:45 to 7:30, weekday mornings, Principal Meade of Eagle Academy in Brooklyn answers phone calls from parents. The questions range from what to do about a young man who is physically aggressive with his mother to how to handle a boy who won't shower. Mr. Meade takes this time to help with the specific issues parents call about, but also to build a deeper respect and trust. Many parents start out (sometimes with good reason) concerned that school principals and teachers don't understand the real-life troubles they face in raising their sons. Mr. Meade makes a point of letting parents know that he grew up in a housing project in a similar neighborhood and that his background is not dissimilar to that of some of his students and their parents. As he explains, the parents "have to see you on the front lines. Otherwise they'll make excuses to discount what you say. If there's a dispute with a white teacher, he or she must be a racist. With a black teacher? 'Didn't grow up where I grew up.'"

Once Mr. Meade establishes that he has personal knowledge of the challenges facing the parents, and even more important, once they see him on the front lines, showing up every day to look after their children with genuine commitment and care, they are more likely to accept him as an authority. With work, parents and students alike will extend that trust to the faculty and the house system. So if, for example, a kid

won't shower when his mother tells him to, she can invoke the authority figures at the school. "If you won't take care of yourself properly, I'm
going to have to call Mr. Meade." And often the rebellious young man
will stand down, because he doesn't want to disappoint his principal or
his house brothers. At the same time, if there is someone at the school
who has created a bond of trust with the young man, then that person
can have a conversation with him about the importance of hygiene or of
talking to one's mother in a respectful way, even when he disagrees with
her point of view. The school and the parents begin to work together
to improve their relationships with the young men, and that brings the
parents a little deeper into their relationship with the school. "The parents are thankful," Mr. Meade says, "to have access to that."

Sometimes it's the parents, not the student, who need assistance to
see a situation in a more productive way. I remember a mother who
called me once, worried because her son had been asked to participate
in an after-school program called Project Read that would require
him to travel on his own to a different neighborhood. She was a single
mother, without another adult in the house to share the responsibility
of deciding when her son was old enough to take new risks and enjoy
new freedoms. I told her, "Mom, you've got to let him grow up!"
She knew and trusted me enough by then to take my opinion into
consideration as she made up her mind about what to allow her son
to do. Our conversation helped her with a tough parenting situation.
It helped her son win a little more independence and participate in
a worthwhile program. But most important, I think, it brought both
mother and son a little more fully into the Eagle family.

We don't replace the family relationships, we reinforce them. And
we do so intending to inspire parents to look for similar support in
other parts of their community. We want them on the lookout for that
trusted neighbor or religious leader or a coach who can benefit their
child. We offer direct help in part to model what offering and finding
good help feels like, so that they will seek it more actively on their own,

and offer it to others when the opportunity arises. If it takes a village to raise a child, then the parents must gather the villagers.

THANKSGIVING

Besides offering direct help to parents in these and other ways, we work to draw our families more fully into the Eagle community with events and celebrations. If you come to our Thanksgiving celebration, a midday communal pot-luck dinner, you will smell the food before you walk into our cafeteria. Coming through the door, you will see table after table all lined up in rows, with students at every one, standing ready to serve homemade food with pride in their faces. If you ask them, "Oh, did your mom make that?" many will be quick to tell you, "No, no! We did it together." Or, "Actually, she taught me how!"

This is especially important for boys in our community, where so many fathers are gone and so many mothers fear losing their boys to the streets. As a result, mothers often coddle their sons. They teach their daughters to cook and clean, to work hard and become self-sufficient, but they are so afraid of losing their boys that they won't push them to be self-sufficient. As Dr. Jawanza Kunjufu, writer and longtime advocate for black boys warns, "We raise our daughters but we love our sons." Some young men in these communities wind up living with their mothers into their thirties and forties, never really developing the independence of men. These mothers don't mean to have that effect, but that can be the result. That's why we make it a rule: every young man comes to the Thanksgiving celebration with a meal he helped to make. And when they do, you can hear them talking together, bragging about who made what and whose dish tastes better. That's the sound of young men cooking their way toward a healthier self-sufficiency.

For some families, this is a chance to share the Thanksgiving traditions they have at home. Other families may have lost the members who would have kept up their traditions, but now our celebration gives them a chance to join in and start making new traditions. Not every family can afford to buy a turkey and bring it to school, so an Eagle representative goes to the local supermarket with our tax-free institution form and places a bulk order. Yvette Crespo describes it this way. "How do we get all these turkeys? I go to Pathmark, get to know the people working there, and then I tell them, 'I need twenty-five turkeys. Can you do something for me? Can you donate to our school?' I show them my no-tax forms. I talk a good game and I flirt a little bit. I'm a hugger—that's Latin culture. So you thank the people at the supermarket for helping the school out, you give them acknowledgment, you bring their business cards back with you to use when we need to order lunch for a staff event at the school. Then we teach our parents about how we got those turkeys, so they can begin networking and bringing back what we all need for our school."

Even if a kid comes to the Thanksgiving celebration from a homeless shelter, one of us will have told him, "You don't walk into someone's house empty-handed. Come in with a soda. It doesn't really matter what you come with, but bring something. In this family, every one of us contributes." We use ceremonies like this to remind our students that it's not enough to focus on what other people can do for you—as tough as some of our young men may have it, many on this planet have it a whole lot worse. We may face some hardships, but we can still be generous. We can come together and create this communal table.

At the celebration, before we eat, our student representatives speak about what they're thankful for. Once again, students and family alike are reminded that they are in a special place, a protected place where they are cared for.

A YEAR OF SHARED CELEBRATIONS

The Thanksgiving and Alumni Day celebration extends the sense of excitement and belonging that parents first felt at the End of the Year ceremony in the spring and at the Stepping Up ceremony when their sons completed Summer Bridge. We have a Winter Holiday celebration and then, come January, when the weather is cold and everyone's dragging, we use that lull to bring in guest speakers. One January we brought in a group of young men, former gang members, to talk about how they wound up incarcerated. There was a snowstorm that day but we still had approximately one hundred parents in attendance. In March, we hold elections for the parent association positions. In May, for Mother's Day, we celebrate our women. And then in June, it's time to celebrate the fathers. Your traditions may differ from ours, but a year structured by tradition helps to reinforce and support our efforts on behalf of our young men.

PLAN FROM THE PARENTS' PERSPECTIVE

Nothing typifies the usual, unambitious parent-school relationship like the parent-teacher association meeting. Consider the ordinary PTA meeting anywhere in the country. Is anything less likely to build the kind of active, helpful, emotionally satisfying community that parents yearn for? The typical PTA meeting is held on a weeknight after classes are done. Why? Because that's what's most convenient for the teachers and administrators. At Eagle we look at PTA meetings from the parents' perspective. A weeknight meeting interrupts dinner. It may mean hiring a babysitter. And how many parents, realistically, can make it to one of those meetings every month?

At Eagle, we have parent meetings only every other month. That way, we can say to the parents at the beginning of the year, "There are only five meetings, but we need you at every one." We hold the meetings on Saturday mornings, at the same time that our students meet with their mentors. Now parent and child are on the same schedule.

To let parents know what they can expect at our meetings, we use every kind of communication we can: flyers in the school, traditional mail, email, texting, word of mouth, messages sent home in their sons' backpacks. Parents call other parents. We announce meetings at our daily town hall. We've had students sing songs on parents' voice mail. We want to be sure we reach everyone, and reach them in ways they might enjoy.

When parents show up for meetings, we praise them in person for coming. Later we'll thank them by email. When they don't come, we'll call the home to ask why. If they are housebound, we will call to thank them for sending us their wonderful son, then brainstorm with them about how they can participate in the Eagle community in other ways.

At meetings, parents discover that the focus is still on what the school can do for them, not just on what they can do for the school. We feed our parents breakfast or lunch. We feature student performances, so they can enjoy some of the best creative work our students have been doing—spoken word, theater, and music. We hold raffles for donated gifts, such as gift certificates to local restaurants and businesses, and when we call the winners to the front of the room, everyone applauds.

The meetings run for two hours. The first hour is the general meeting with all the parents together, while the second is broken down by grades so that parents know they will be getting useful information targeted to their son's experience—no eleventh graders' parent wants to hear about the new ninth grade math teacher. But our meetings are not just school business. Our goal is to make parent meetings into events that parents would want to attend even if they didn't have students at our school. We have guest speakers and seminars on topics parents have told us that they need to know about—tips on job hunting and maintaining credit, strategies for adults wishing to take out a mortgage or earn a college degree. We have had guests from the district attorney's office come in to discuss the dangers kids may find on the Internet. We have offered our parents the same etiquette class we make available to our students. Tracy Lewis, one of our first parent coordinators, has run stress and health workshops in which she teaches light meditation, and the parents loved it. We are constantly trying to figure out how to support our parents, how to meet their needs a little better so they can meet their sons' needs a little better. Our parents participate at such an extraordinary level—80 to 85 percent—not just because we ask them to sign contracts of participation, but because we work to make participating in the school a way to improve their own lives.

It may seem, again, as if we're offering our parents a simple trade: we'll make this enjoyable for you, but you have to show up and participate. But there's more to it. When they show up, we ask them to commit to participate, but only, at first, in a very small way: to volunteer for an hour, or to attend one committee meeting. Their time may be short, but if they will volunteer for one brief, specific task, it gives the parent coordinator or other volunteers or staff members a chance to talk with them. Only then can we learn what a new volunteer needs and what they might have to offer—who they might know or what resources they might be able to access for the school. This parent might work for a company that would like to be part of our mentoring program. That parent might have grown up with a politician or artist who would like to come speak to our students. Another parent might make us aware of a challenge he or she is facing, which could be the basis for a new seminar or workshop in the future. Some parents might be able to volunteer during the day. Others might never be able to get away from work during the day, but could come at night or on weekends. We have to get to know our parents before we can appreciate—and then, yes, finally, make use of—the amazing resources they represent. And as we find ways for our parents to participate, we draw them closer into the community, engage them more in their sons' education, and show them as best we can what it feels like to be part of a mutually beneficial community in the service of shared goals. In a community like that, when the school has a need, the parent coordinator can send out a message saying, "The principal really needs X," and our parents will step up and make sure it happens.

A PLACE OF WELCOME

Through all the gatherings and meetings, we remind our parents that there is a room in the school where they are always invited. When we first started at Eagle Academy, sharing space with another school, we didn't have a parent center. All I could give a parent coordinator at first was a large closet, but the vision from the beginning was a space where parents as well as staff could stop by informally. In time, we were able to have a room with a conference table, and offer parents coffee, hot chocolate, and tea. We got them a refrigerator, a printer, a fax machine and scanner, and other items that would make it inviting and useful for them to stop by. Parents would drop in to ask how their son was doing. Sometimes staff members would stop in when they needed a little time away from the teacher's lounge.

At one parent meeting, a mother mentioned that she liked to crochet. Another said, "So do I." Another said, "I'd like to know how." Someone suggested that if we started a parent group to crochet baby blankets, we could give them to St. Barnabus, the nearby hospital. That crochet group began to meet two or three times a week in the parent center and it became a chance for the parents to get a little relief, a little conversation time. Some of the staff members heard about the group and they came by to learn how to crochet, both women and men. Now the parents had a deeper sense of community, meeting and talking, where those in need could transmit practical knowledge and share vital emotional support.

In a similar way, Bronx principal Jonathan Foy started a men's council for Eagle fathers and other male caregivers, and found that men who weren't participating in the school in other ways, or who volunteered time but had little to say, became loyal to the men's group and opened up in ways they wouldn't elsewhere.

The benefits were profound. The young men got to see not just mothers but a group of father figures who felt it was worthwhile to be involved in the life of the school. As a result of interacting in that group, the parent coordinator learned a great deal about what was going on at home for some of our students, for example, whose parents were unemployed, or who'd had a recent death in their family.

In a healthy, close community everyone keeps his or her eyes open and everyone contributes when they can. Having the parents, teachers, and staff socializing together in the crochet group, the men's group, and other parent-center activities helped us to tap into the benefits of community. For example, the children were reminded that the kitchen staff is not "the help." The people serving meals to our children are in a position to notice when a young man is going back for thirds or fourths. If they have gotten to know our students and won their trust, even in small ways, they may be able to ask, "Are you eating at home?" If they notice what might be a more serious concern for that young man, they can make others in the school aware of it.

In the same way, the school safety officer who is employed at the front desk can engage kids in conversation. *Do you know what not to say when police approach?* Students can see by her badge that she knows what she's talking about, and she has the opportunity to speak to kids one on one. That's a whole lot more powerful for a young man than a lecture on safety. Those are the kinds of things that come about when there is a chance for people who normally see one another in a formal setting to come together and socialize informally. The guard at the front desk can be a sypathetic ear. The server in the cafeteria can be a confidant and a pair of wise, watchful eyes. We are all educators, all parents.

THE CHALLENGES OF MARRIAGE

One strength of the community that raised me, back on 223rd Street in Queens, was that there were so many two-parent households. I'm grateful that my parents stuck it out through our childhoods, but on our block they did not stand out as some unique example of parental commitment. Did that mean the relationships were perfect or without strife? Of course not. There were all the usual tensions. For my mom and dad, the number one argument was about money. Some nights there was a lot of yelling. The bedroom door would be closed but we could hear it. Those disagreements would have bothered any kid. To this day I still remember that feeling.

Already then, and even more so now, the celebrity culture was full of messages that discouraged sticking together. You could get the feeling that marriage was something to be tried on when the mood struck, like new clothes. *Tired of this outfit? Try something else.* On my block, though, I got a different message: *Stay with your family.* We were shown the value of persistence, resilience, stick-to-it-iveness. Some of that came from religious faith. Some of it I saw with my father and the men on our block. They showed us by their own actions and their words, saying, "Marriage gets very frustrating sometimes, sometimes you argue, but there are things you don't do. When you get really frustrated, you have to walk away. Get out of the house." And most important: "You don't leave your kids."

My parents were an inspiration to me, but what I didn't understand until later was how much they depended on the other marriages on the block that were an inspiration for them. The wives got together to talk about the challenges of marriage and to help each other out. The husbands had the guy talk in the living room. Growing up, I felt like there were always three, four, five people visiting our house, playing cards, throwing something on the grill, laughing, talking over a drink. It was the brotherhood, the sisterhood, what a community is supposed to be. My mother says that when other families had trouble, there was always someone to wrap their arms around them, share what they were going through, and encourage them. When one neighbor went through some hard times with her husband, she would sneak over to our house in the middle of the night. My mother was always there to give counsel and share her own stories, and she wouldn't be the only one. There was light radiating out all over the place. So the neighbor going through hard times had somewhere to go. She didn't just take off running in the streets and do something that would make hard times even worse.

This is the vision I have for our parent community. It's not just a way to get volunteers for the school, but a place where parents can find others they can go to—who can offer an ear or a touch, give them confidence that they can speak about private things and the listener won't spread their business everywhere. As Yvette Crespo describes it, "It's about letting our hair down and being women and mothers and men and fathers who go through all these things, who feel all these things. It's about empowering ourselves. It's a place where someone can come and say, 'Can I speak to you? I'm going through something,' 'My son is in trouble,' or 'My man has cancer,' or 'My mother just passed.' A place where we can find some empathy, some humor, some acknowledgment that we're all in this pot together as parents. And if we can help one another, it will resonate with our young men."

If parents in need can find other adults to connect with, helpful information, or a shoulder to cry on when they are going through hard life changes, they will make better decisions for themselves and act out of desperation less often. That means more sons able to concentrate on becoming good young men, not worrying how they're going to live once the roof has fallen down around them.

The larger point is that parents can be the essential influence on their children's success—but to be the best influences they can be, they need to support one another. That support doesn't need to look like what we have at Eagle, and it doesn't need to be organized around the life of a school. We have had a knitting circle, but it could just as well be a gardening group, a book club, or a weekly bowling night. We work to make the school a central part of the community for all of our students, but efforts to gather and support parents could just as well be organized around a house of worship, a community center, a block or building association, or anything else that brings families together.

Wherever it may be, I suspect it will be helpful to follow the same basic steps we learned to take at Eagle. First, find a way to gather parents somewhere that they will have the chance to talk about their own lives. Let their needs, not any larger plans for supporting young men, come first. Some will benefit from the chance to ask for help. Some will benefit from the chance to give it. Encourage conversations about what each parent needs in order to succeed as a parent, and to help their children succeed, and work to learn what each parent who shows up might have to offer. A group of parents who all want their young men to thrive is already a bit like an extended family, and with a regular chance to meet and talk and some leadership to help sort out who can contribute what, that family feeling can grow into a mutually supportive and reinforced community.

CHAPTER SIX

REGRET CAN KILL YOU

Mentoring Manhood

Modou Blake seemed to have it all going for him. A promising student, smart and responsible, he was the child of parents who had come from Antigua, in the Caribbean, with a solid marriage, strong traditional values, and a deep commitment to helping their children make a better life. He played the piano and sang, and one of the first times he met his assigned mentor, Errol Pierre, it was after a performance Modou gave at the winter holiday celebration. He seemed ripe for success.

Soon, though, Modou's grades collapsed. He became so unresponsive in class that one of his teachers, frustrated and angry, lost control and screamed at him. His mother was also at her wit's end—she told Mr. Pierre that her son was silent all day, defiant for the sake of being defiant, then up all night on his cell phone and his computer.

One day in the middle of class, a house brother heard Modou

listening to music and yanked his headphones out of his ears. Modou punched him. The dean of students called his mentor, asking for help. Here was a student with a strong, supportive family, a young man whom teachers expected to do well, and yet just when it seemed he had begun to soar, he was in danger of crashing to the ground. What was going wrong?

When a young man has a lot going right for him, it can be that much harder for others to see what's going wrong. I want to compare Modou's story to that of Rudy Coombs, one of the mentors who worked with our students in the Bronx. Rudy's difficulties were much easier to spot, and they shed light on the difficulties many young men face in grasping opportunities, and the difference a mentor can make when they start to go wrong.

Rudy grew up in the South Bronx a generation before Eagle Academy was established there. He explains, "I went to three high schools and I was kicked out of two of them. I told my high school guidance counselor that I wanted to be a lawyer, but he said I should take vocational courses. I ended up working with steel machines. It was very frustrating. I was involved with the gangs, the drug dealing, and all kinds of crazy nonsense.

"At seventeen, I was hanging out with a guy who was twenty-five, a burglar. He was teaching me a trade—the trade of being a burglar. I thought, sure, we could do that and get away with it—he's a grown man, he'll teach me how. There was no one to say, 'Hey, Rudy, this is not cool.'

"The one thing I had: I played basketball. I was very good at basketball. I won a scholarship, a full four-year scholarship, to go to college in Georgia. People started talking to me about the Ku Klux Klan and all the other [racist] stuff down there, and I thought, 'I'm not going down there!'"

Rudy was a member of the local community center, where he played basketball and pool in the evenings. Over the years, he had become close to the center's director, and he told the older man about his decision to turn down the scholarship. "The director sat me down and said, 'Rudy, look, just go down to Georgia and check it out. If you don't like it, you always have the opportunity to come back. But you're not going to take a four-year scholarship and just throw it away. Go down there—do it for me. For me! Go down and check it out.'

"So I went, because he said so. It was the best thing that ever happened to me. They actually cared about me studying, finding fellowship with the other students, and getting good grades. When they found academic areas I lacked in, they got me tutors. The tutors would stick with me because they wanted me to play basketball. I had never been to a school where they actually cared.

"In the summers, I stayed down there for summer school. When I graduated, I cried tears of joy because here was a kid from the South Bronx receiving a bachelor of arts degree in sociology. I had never even dreamed of that."

Rudy had grown up in some of the most dangerous conditions a young man can face—a crime-ridden neighborhood; peers headed for academic failure and in many cases prison; teachers and counselors with little stake in his success as a student—and he'd received an opportunity to rise above those conditions. But when he almost blew that chance, it was not because of his neighborhood, his peers, his parents, or even his teachers. By that point, the most serious danger was not outside of him, but inside. He had lived in a toxic environment for so long, it had damaged his judgment. In that state, he imagined that apprenticing as a burglar was good preparation for the future. He imagined that a rural college campus could be dangerous, but his neighborhood was safe. Most of all, he imagined that the best thing he could do for himself was to keep his life as it was. It was as if he saw everything upside-down.

What Rudy needed was someone he could trust to show him

clearly where he was, where he had the chance to go, and how to get there: a mentor. Chris Merritt, a former Eagle student, defined the need for a mentor in this way: "A young man without a mentor is like an explorer without a map." Young men in the teenage years still have the chance to seize opportunities, to go beyond the life they have known so far and to get to somewhere that will fulfill their potential and their dreams, but very often, even when they don't face the kind of challenges that Rudy faced, they don't know how to fulfill their promise. They don't see the value in the opportunities they get. They lack the courage to take the risks they need to take, especially if it means leaving the small neighborhood they have known best. If they do set out on their journey, they often head in the wrong direction. They need a trusted guide with an outsider's perspective, who can help them make their way from here to there—someone who feels, *I don't care how it looks to anyone else; I know this young man can make it and I'm going to be there to help see him through.*

These days, of course, *mentor* is a word we hear all the time, a buzzword. "At our school, everybody is a mentor!" Teachers are mentors to their students, for example. But at Eagle, when we reference mentorship, we have a more systematic and ongoing sort of guidance in mind. In any classroom, sure, a few students will draw closer to the teacher, but it's physically impossible for the teacher to mentor every student in a class in the way I will describe. That's not a criticism of teachers. There simply aren't enough hours in the day for teachers to mentor all or even many of the students they teach. If every student is going to have a mentor, you can't ask the faculty to take care of it. You have to get the community involved.

MORE THAN A PICTURE

Our approach to mentoring developed over time, through trial and error. We started in 2004, drawing most of our first mentors from the One Hundred Black Men. Early on, the emphasis was on mentors giving young men a picture of what was possible, following the approach that "they will be what they see." A mentor would take a student to a Knicks game, a movie, or Broadway show, and then to a restaurant. He would make sure to talk about his career. The idea was to say, *I've achieved this, and you can achieve it, too.*

We came to understand that for many of our young men, a picture of success, even a picture with a man's face that looks like theirs, is not enough. They need not just inspiration but a practical guide, a loyal companion on the journey, someone who will help when they are struggling. Keenan Williams, a young investment banker who volunteers as one of our mentors, explains, "It's not enough to show what's possible. You have to show *how*. You have to point out when a young man is getting in his own way, when he's not using the resources that are right in front of him, and when he's accepting faulty guidance from people who can't see his potential or don't support it."

That was the kind of practical guidance that Modou, the struggling student I introduced at the beginning of this chapter, needed, despite having many advantages that Rudy Coombs, who won the basketball scholarship, lacked. Modou found that guidance with Errol Pierre, whose own childhood and later success gave him a map of the journey that Modou needed to take.

Mr. Pierre explains, "Modou and I have a bond because his parents are from Antigua, in the West Indies, and my parents grew up in Haiti. I'd spoken to his mother two or three times, first at the winter holiday celebration and then after her son came to my workplace for an event. Each time, I saw a lot of my mom in her. Her rules were her rules, and her children had to respect them, no ifs, ands, or buts. Her children had to keep up their grades. Talk with parents was a one-way conversation. Talking back was not allowed."

Modou felt that his parents didn't understand American culture. They didn't realize that in this country, people had open conversations. They didn't understand the new communications technology. He tried telling his mother, "You're behind the times! People go on Facebook at night!" He struggled with living up to their expectations while still fitting in at school. His attitude was: *My mom doesn't get it, so I'm not going to listen to her anymore. And if my teacher gives me a hard time, I'm not going to listen to her, either.* He was caught between two worlds, and his solution was to shut down and ignore rules and grades as much as he could. His plan seemed to be that he would keep his headphones tight in his ears and his eyes on his Facebook page until he got to college.

Over several conversations, Mr. Pierre told him, "I know how it is. My parents are like that, too. It would be a great achievement for my dad if he could even operate a cell phone. I know how frustrating that is. But they won't change, not much. So as long as you're under her roof and your parents are paying for the electricity and the gas, you're going to have to follow her rules. If you hate it that bad, if it's the worst thing in the world, what are you doing to make sure you get the first opportunity to make up your own rules? Maybe it's ice cream for dinner and video games all night, fine—what are you doing to get there?

"You say college is how you get away, but you have to understand that to get to college you need to have good grades or you'll be commuting to a community college—and then you'll find yourself back at home, still under your mother's roof. For your own sake, to get what you want, you need good grades. So every day, what can you do to align with that goal?"

As their conversations continued, Mr. Pierre encouraged him to try to see that what his parents did, even when it was annoying or seemed uninformed, was coming straight from love. They talked about how Modou's parents came to America for his sake, and what they had to do to get here. They tried together to imagine what Modou's life would have been like, how his opportunities might have been limited, if his family hadn't sacrificed to bring him from Antigua to New York City.

"Your mother is someone on your team," Mr. Pierre told him, repeatedly.

"Yeah, I know, I know . . ." Modou answered.

"No, you really have to know this, you have to understand this. She's not fighting against you. She wants your life to be better than hers."

That's one of the most important messages that a mentor can reinforce. *Dream high. Go beyond those around you. The sky's the limit.* Mentor Keenan Williams describes it this way: "I say to them, 'I'm only eight years older than you, and if you do what I did, you can have what I have. Do I want that? No. I want you to be even better than me.'"

At the same time that Mr. Pierre was working to show Modou a more productive way of thinking about his parents, he tried to help Modou show his parents how they could better help their son succeed. When Modou was struggling in physics, his teacher offered to meet after school on Fridays, but the young man was expected to go to church with his family on Friday nights. Mr. Pierre called his mother and told her, "The teacher said Modou didn't show up for tutoring. What do you think we should do?" Approached in that way, not criticized as ignorant or told what to do, his mother responded, "We may have to figure out how to change his schedule." She and her son were able to have a less charged, more productive conversation about making some changes to help reach goals that mattered to all of them.

At Eagle, the burden of this sort of change does not fall solely on the mentor. All the partners are involved. Modou's parents encouraged the relationship between their son and his mentor, and his mother called the dean of students when she felt she couldn't handle Modou's behavior. His teachers and the dean, who also acted as the mentoring coordinator, had their eyes on the young man, and both continued to talk with him in school and to provide Mr. Pierre with updates. Modou's house brothers offered their support as well—in fact, it was a high-achieving house brother, active in the school, who had taken Mr. Pierre aside after a Saturday group-mentoring session and told him about the fight over the headphones. But it was Mr. Pierre who had the chance to act as guide.

MAKING A MATCH

When I was growing up, I was fortunate to have my father closely involved in my life, but he understood that even a young man with a good father still needs other mentors. He also understood that few teenagers will find mentors on their own. My father made a point of introducing me to friends of his, who took time out to talk with me about my interests and the choices I was making. (*Hey, Dave, it's good to see you again. You still interested in the law? Let me talk to you about a couple of things you're going to need to do.*) But many young men don't have a father fully involved in their lives, and many parents and teachers don't know how to facilitate that kind of relationship. That's a double loss—the young man loses both the guidance of a father and the guidance of the mentors the father might have helped him to find.

A lot of the work of mentoring is preparation—building the relationship of trust before a young man faces a fateful decision or an opportunity that could change his life. So although young people need adults in their lives to make the introductions, only the mentee can decide who he can trust. It's not possible for an adult to *assign* a young person a mentor. The young person has to feel drawn to that person and able to talk with him.

When we started mentoring at Eagle, we assigned mentors to students, but too often we made poor matches. Then, on top of the challenge of finding enough mentors for every student, we had the challenge of what to do when a student didn't click with the mentor we chose for him. At the same time, as we expanded, it was difficult to find individual mentors for thousands of students. With some outside guidance, we decided to shift to a group mentoring approach. Now our mentoring begins in classroom-sized groups. Four mentors come in one Saturday a month and meet with twenty students for a shared discussion. The topics evolve over the years of middle and high school, covering young men's personal and cultural identity, to community service, preparation for college, work, and work internships. We have found that students open up faster with new mentors and are quicker to feel trust when they hear their peers express some of their own concerns and questions.

Our mentors don't have to make personal connections with all twenty students in the room—if they can connect with five or so each, then every student will have both a group mentoring experience and one mentor who connects with him personally. Often mentors are surprised by which kids pick them out, and what the students will tell them, later, was the most important way the mentor influenced the student. So rather than trying to craft the perfect match, it's better to expose a young person to several potential mentors, and let the young man feel his way to one that is right for him.

Eagle mentor Kendrick Harris, an attorney, gives the example of a Saturday, early in the semester, when he was part of a mentoring group and one of the art teachers came into the room to observe. Later, she pulled him aside to say, "That young man you were talking with just now, he's always withdrawn. We've had trouble with him reeking of weed. He only seems to come to school for art. I've never seen him interact with anyone like he did with you! You really should reach out to him." No one knew in advance that the young man would connect with Kendrick; Kendrick didn't realize that their connection was exceptional in the boy's life until the teacher let him know. So if we are going to make useful matches, our young men need adults to set the process in motion, but then to step back, observe what works, and be surprised.

The match between Modou and Mr. Pierre was also something we all discovered along the way. Modou had been approached by several teachers and the dean of students, all of whom had tried to show that they would welcome a more personal conversation. They were sincerely interested in him, but they didn't feel to him like the guides he was looking for. The dean picked out Mr. Pierre as one potential mentor, but it was only the right choice because it felt right to Modou. As in so much of our work with young men, we don't know exactly when the light will go on, and we don't necessarily ever find out why. But we are not psychologists, and it's not our job to explain the precise emotional workings of the young men we try to help. Instead, we need to keep creating opportunities for them to make positive connections, and let them step up and make use of what's right.

We have gathered our mentors over the years by letting men in the community know that we have a need and asking them to commit to an ongoing relationship on a reliable schedule. We have spread the word at businesses that have relationships with Eagle, through churches and community organizations, and by talking about our need for mentors in the media and in private conversations—in other words, wherever we can. You can do the same on behalf of a young man. Most people will be flattered to be asked to play such a role in a young man's life, and if you explain the kind of relationship you are hoping for, they will understand the type of commitment you're asking them to make.

CREDIBILITY

For young men, the first test of a mentor is credibility. When Eagles and potential mentors are introduced, our students are asking themselves and each other, *Is this guy okay? Does he know what it's like to be one of us? Is he legit?* If they're willing to talk to the potential mentor at all, they will want personal information: *Where do you live? Where do your kids go to school?* They are really saying, *Show me what you have gone through that's similar to what I've gone through. Can you understand a life like mine, or have you just heard about it? Will you be able to listen to me and not crowd me with judgments?*

This is not simply a matter of making kids comfortable. Our young men are right to assume that if a mentor is going to be helpful, he's going to have to show them the entire map—not just where they are trying to get, the ultimate success, but where they started out, the life they know. Aaron Barnette, who was the first director of our mentoring program before he became dean of students, explains, "The way we impact the lives of young men is that we can relate to the things they're going through. I wouldn't be able to give the advice I give them had I not gone through those trials myself. A lot of things they glamorize, such as the street life, are what they see on television and a lot of that is fantasy anyway. They need someone to say, *I thought that was reality, too, and I went through my phases in life, I made the same mistakes, and you know what? It's not as glamorous as you think.* It means something to them to have someone in my position admit that.

"That's one of the ways mentors are different from parents. As parents, we don't always want to keep it one hundred percent real with our kids because we want to shield our own children. But the way the world is, it's not all sugar and cream. Often as parents you may have made the same mistakes they are in danger of making, but you don't honestly share that with your children. My son is thirteen and I have not shared with him some of the things I have shared with these guys here at Eagle."

BE THEIR ANGEL

Another test of credibility, and another way that mentors must act differently from parents, is that they have to focus on the young person's concerns and perspective, not on the parents' short-term goals. Some first-time mentors are surprised, when they meet ninth and tenth graders, to feel a strong impulse to make the young men act more presentable: *Sit up straight! Speak up! Pull up your pants! Take off your coat when you come inside!* Most young men already get plenty of that. They don't need another father or uncle or brother or teacher telling them how to comport themselves, they need a grown man on their side, an angel on their shoulder who is focused first of all on their journey to manhood, not their wrinkled shirt and mismatched socks. There will come a time later to talk about the importance of how they present themselves to the world, but it can't come first.

For the same reason, Eagle mentors are discouraged from giving gifts. If a mentee is only showing up to get some material thing that he wants, or that his parent hopes the mentor will buy, it will be that much harder to have a true meeting of the minds. The goal is for the mentor to become the adult to whom a young man can tell the serious things he feels he can't tell other adults. Otherwise, he may only tell his friends, who are likely to know as little as he does.

Because mentors need to get so close to the young men they work with, they run a risk of seeming to crowd out the parents. When mentoring a young man with a father active in his life, it is crucial to leave a respectful space for the father. Although Eagle mentors often sit with mentees who lack fathers at Eagle events, I encourage mentors to leave that special place for the fathers who are there. Until the relationship is well established with the family, it can be important at public events to greet the father first, praising his son and observing how important he is to the young man. The mentor needs to be the one to make clear that he is there not to replace anybody, but only to offer reinforcement.

Most of the time, when parents see a mentor helping to solve practical problems and get results—helping their son to connect with teachers, to improve his behavior, to raise his grades, or to have experiences that inspire and energize him—then the parents will almost always become comfortable having a mentor in their young man's life.

SHOW DEDICATION

After credibility, young men will be looking for dedication. Who shows up on time for mentor meetings? Who answers their emails? What do other students report about the reliability of these men who claim to be role models? Volunteer mentors sometimes suffer from the same flightiness you find with volunteers at soup kitchens: everyone feels good volunteering on Thanksgiving and Christmas, but a kitchen needs cooks and servers year-round, even after the Christmas trees have been put out on the street and it's bitter cold outside.

Our young men are often hyperalert for warning signs that the mentors who show up full of enthusiasm in September, when the school year begins, may be losing interest a few months later, such as not taking their calls. Young men who have no father in their lives, or whose fathers are around much less than they would hope, already expect to be let down. Just as they are quick to sense whether or not a teacher cares, they can sense when a mentor cares, and if he doesn't, then you have lost them. They don't want to be disappointed again. It comes down to the combination of caring and security: they need real men who show up to demonstrate their commitment by giving real time.

One of the most impressive things to our young men is to come to school on a Saturday and see these accomplished men walking the halls in their casual clothes and attending the mentoring sessions. Word will get around—*Did you hear, this one drove all the way from his country home! He drove eighty miles just to work with us!* The young men understand the commitment when they see it: *These men are consistent, and they are here. This is something special—and I must be special because they're coming here for me.*

PLAY

Our mentors don't just have discussions with the boys on Saturdays or take them to meals or events, they play sports together. It may be basketball, Ping-Pong—it doesn't really matter what, as long as it's play. This gives the mentors the chance to be boyish again with boys who still have so much of the youthful magic, and it gives the young men a chance to see that grown, successful men are still little boys at heart, still looking to have fun. I remember when Magic Johnson retired from basketball. He said it wasn't the game he would miss as much as the camaraderie with the guys in the locker room, that place where you can still laugh deep laughs.

Over time, as credibility and trust slowly build, even young men who have been disappointed in the past can open up. For some of the mentors, this can be almost frightening. They realize how much these young men look up to them, and how big a role they are being asked to play in helping the young men achieve their dreams. One mentor explains, "I've had kids who are ashamed to tell me what's going wrong in their classes. They hide from me and I have to follow them, probe a little: 'Hey, where've you been? You haven't called me.' You chip away and they say, 'Physics is really tough, I'm failing, I'm sorry.' They apologize to you. That's when I ask, 'Are you doing everything you can? I'll speak to your principal, your teachers, to find out if there is more you can do. Is there after-school tutoring? Are you giving one hundred percent? I'm not going to yell at you. I just want to understand if you're doing your best. If you are not doing everything in your power, then let's find out together what more you can do.'"

THE SKILLS FOR THE JOURNEY

Mentoring is powerful because it can provide a young man with exactly the practical skills, fresh perspectives, or emotional support he needs, at just the right time. After Modou got into a scuffle with his fellow student—his first fight, not the behavior anyone expected from him—Errol helped him to understand how he had gotten into the fight, and how he might avoid situations like that in the future. Errol told him he wanted to understand what had happened. Modou said that he was having a bad day, didn't feel like being in school, and just wanted to listen to his iPod, though that was against school rules. When the other student pulled his headphones out, Modou was angry that the other boy had violated his space and touched him. "He made me mad!" Modou explained.

"No one can *make* you mad," his mentor replied. "Don't give the other guy that power over you. Even in that moment, there are a lot of things that you control. But the second you give that up, you're giving them control of you. Now they have *made* you mad. So even when the other guy is in the wrong and you feel upset about it, you need to make sure he sees who is in control of your actions."

Modou needed guidance in handling his emotions, but the range of skills and insights that our students gain from their mentors is very wide. Other students need help understanding the educational choices they face in high school. Mentor Tyrone McKinney tells the story of hearing several mentees in his group complaining after the end of a grading period about a computer course they were finding difficult. These were ninth graders who were comfortable with video-gaming platforms such as Playstations and Xboxes, and who knew a lot, compared to their parents, about how to navigate the Internet and maximize the use of their cell phones. Confronted with Microsoft business programs, though, they were surprised to find the class work difficult. Some had expected the course to be a pushover and now they told Tyrone that they weren't going to take it seriously anymore.

Tyrone asked his mentees to tell him more about what they were studying in the computing class, and realized it was sophisticated material, almost at the level of the Microsoft certification that he had taken as part of his own professional development. He explained to his mentoring group, "You couldn't know this based on your experiences with your friends and at school, but I'm out in the work world, and I can tell you that this course offers skills you will need in the corporate environment or to become an entrepreneur. These are skills you can take with you to college and on your journey into the workforce. This is worth your time." Once they were shown how the course represented a practical opportunity and were encouraged by a mentor they respected, many of the students applied themselves in the class with new vigor.

Sometimes mentors can show young men how to conduct themselves in a part of the adult world for which they feel unqualified. Eagle mentor Keenan Williams tells the story of a young man who loved high-end cars, though most of what he knew about them came from hip-hop videos. For this young man, material success meant television images of rappers. Keenan wanted to widen his sense of what was possible, so he took him for a walk in Manhattan to see the real thing at the Park Avenue car dealerships.

At the Audi dealership, his mentee was excited to sit in an R8 sports car. Then they walked up to the Ferrari showroom, and the young man hesitated to go in the door. But with a little encouragement, while Keenan chatted with the salesman, he sat in a Ferrari hatchback, very impressed.

Across the street was Mercedes-Benz. In the showroom they had the new Maybach, a car with a base retail price of about four hundred thousand dollars. A salesman came up to them at the door, very welcoming, but even after Keenan and the salesman chatted for a couple of minutes, Keenan had to nudge the young man to walk farther into the dealership. Approaching the car, the kid grew so nervous that he started to shake. The salesman, a white man in his fifties, opened the door for him, but he couldn't move.

It was a crisis of self-worth. *Do I deserve to be here?* It doesn't take a Mercedes-Benz dealership to provoke that kind of reaction in a young man who rarely leaves the area where he's spent most of his life. It could be sitting down to eat in a restaurant just one step above what he's known before.

The three men stood together. The salesman said, "Listen, son, it's just a car." It took a few minutes before the young man could sit in the seat. Then he studied all the details—the suede floor, the umbrella built into the door. Afterward, the salesman said, "Please come back again."

Now the young man could begin to picture himself in one of his dream cars without becoming a rapper or a drug dealer. He wanted to know how his mentor had talked to the salesman to get such a warm welcome. "How did you do that? How did you get him to act that way?" It was his first time realizing that it's not just a question of a man putting on a suit, but of learning how a man in a suit operates, what it means to be articulate and effective. And he had glimpsed some of what he would need to get there. That is the essence of mentoring—exposing a young person to parts of the world they will need to navigate if they are to reach their dreams.

REGRET CAN KILL YOU

Kendrick Harris, who mentors students at Eagle Academy, tells this story.

"I had mentored Alfred for three years, including helping him to build his résumé of experiences for college applications. Most kids in his neighborhood in Brooklyn had never traveled beyond ten square blocks. They hadn't even been to the Bronx or Harlem. But Eagle helps to organize opportunities for students to travel, and Alfred got a chance to go to Australia. Then for some reason, people in his neighborhood started to influence him against it. They asked him, 'Why do you want to go there? There are no black people there.'

"His mother has gotten to know me as his mentor, and she called me up to say that he was not going. I asked her to put him on the phone.

"'What's going on?' I asked him.

"'I don't know if I should I go. People say I might not like it. And I have to write these reports.'

"I'd been his mentor long enough that the barriers to conversation were low. I told him, 'Yo, Alfred, you are bugging. But I'm not going to let you be afraid. You are not going to let some people stop you from taking this opportunity. I don't care if you get to go again in your life, you'll never be sixteen in Australia, ever.' We had been together long enough that I felt comfortable. I hollered at him—I'm passionate and he knows that. I knew he wouldn't feel intimidated. Then I told him, 'The most important thing I want to save you from is regret. You're going to regret not taking this opportunity, and regret will kill you. Regret drives people insane.'

"Finally, he went on the trip. He came back and said, 'Thank you so much. I saw so much I never knew—I got to meet aborigines. I swam in the Great Barrier Reef. I went to the opera house. There were even black girls there, the prettiest black girls I'd ever seen.' Then I knew that he'd discovered that sometimes the people in your home environment, out of their own confusion and fear, can make a young person go against his own best interests. And that he'd remember that his entire life."

TIE THE TIE

A mentor's job is not just to position himself to give guidance at important, potentially life-changing moments. It is to provide a slow, patient introduction to manhood. Aaron Barnette says, "It's the little things people overlook that these guys need guidance on. We have a Saturday session where the mentors teach the kids how to tie a tie. Afterward there are always kids who come to me and say, 'I know how to tie my tie now!' That may seem like something small to somebody else, but to me, seeing the look on that young man's face is very powerful, because my dad taught me how to tie my tie. And I can only imagine what it would be like if he hadn't, and I had nobody to do that for me."

It's extraordinary how many men involved with Eagle have their own stories about who taught them to tie a tie, and what it meant for them to do that for a younger man. Mentor Tyrone McKinney agrees. "Too many inner-city young men only put on a tie when it's too late—for a job interview or when they're buried. I didn't know how to do a Windsor knot until after college. I wore a clip-on, so I only had to straighten it up. Only a handful of my friends actually knew how. Early on in my career, I wasn't tying my ties right. A friend of mine, a Caucasian man, stood in front of me and made sure I knew how to tie a tie. So at Eagle, they don't allow pre-knotted ties or clip-ons. And when Eagle holds their 'tie the tie' ceremony, I look at it as a rite of passage to manhood."

It's not just the ties. Talking with young men about something as simple as the proper deodorant to wear at the age of fourteen—when they're too old to borrow their mother's—or what happens to their gums as they get older if they don't take care of their teeth, or what to do now that there are hairs all over their body, can make an enormous difference—because the mentor is being open to whatever the young man needs at that particular moment, whatever the next step may be in the emotional and interpersonal challenges of his life. And in time that openness can lead to conversations about sexual conduct, homosexuality, drug use, addictions, and lack of empathy for oneself—questions of profound importance for men.

A WIDER PERSPECTIVE

Beginning with discussions about their own changing bodies and experiences, mentors move on to encourage the expectation that an educated and responsible man is aware of the larger world around him, the pressing issues in his community, his country, and his world. In group mentoring sessions, our students talk about current events that are relevant to their lives, from local political questions to violence in the community. The goal is to show that as grown members of their communities, they will be expected to explore their feelings and formulate their points of view through discussion with others.

Some of our mentors are able to involve their mentees in projects related to their own work. One mentor in the health-care field brought mentees to compete in a program for college students where students used data from the Centers for Disease Control to look for evidence of disparities in health and health care in their own communities. It was not only a chance for high school students to engage in college-level work as an extracurricular project, but also to start looking around their own neighborhoods and seeing that there were pressing health-care issues, including diabetes and asthma. The students were then asked to come up with ways to increase awareness within the community, and to meet with members of health-care organizations and present their ideas. For some, it was the first time they had entered corporate offices, let alone presented their original ideas to professionals.

Taking a very different approach, several Eagle mentors use a discussion exercise about gender roles for parents. At a group mentoring meeting, they will ask students to brainstorm about the roles played by mothers and fathers in a typical family. Students often give a long list of roles for mothers, and just a few for fathers: discipline the kids, earn money, and watch football. The mentors will describe this family arrangement as like a beehive—the females are the queen bees, the males are drones providing a few fixed services. In a beehive, your mother tells you what to do, what to clean, and so on, and then you start dating and you look for someone to replace her. Then the mentors will ask students to imagine that they are going to be fathers. What roles would they like to play? Many of the young men will pick roles they had assigned to mothers, including emotional involvement with the kids, nurturing them, and helping them develop for the future. So what would need to change, we ask them, if we men want to be more involved fathers?

These are just a few examples of ways that mentors can get their mentees thinking and talking about the larger world they are entering as men, and how they might help to shape it. This kind of talk—exploring their surroundings, questioning their perceptions and their feelings, imagining the personal and the global consequences of their beliefs and choices—is one antidote to the upside-down thinking that can spoil a young man's judgment and cost him crucial opportunities.

BUILDING YOUR OWN MAN

Young men benefit from time with their mentors even when there is no agenda or larger life lesson. Simply spending informal time with successful men who care about them can give mentees a chance to build their own sense of who they want to become. One mentor may wear cuff links and a pocket square in his suit coat, and a young man may realize, *I could dress like that one day—he's a man like me, but he dresses like that.* Another mentor may wear jeans and sneakers, the same sneakers some kids wear, but he's an attorney. A young man might come to understand, *I don't have to lose who I am, there's room for me to expand without giving up my own style.* Former Eagle student Michael Mayo put it this way: "I don't believe anybody knows what a man is supposed to be. You're building your own man as you go along. I look for things that I like, certain character traits in certain men, and I adapt them in my life, for me. Having mentors gave me character traits to adapt."

A LIFE IN MENTORING

The men who offer themselves as the type of mentors I have been describing, guides who can help young men get from here to there, do it for many reasons. Some do it because they were mentored themselves and they know what a difference it can make. Some participate because they were never mentored and they know how hard it is to go it alone. Some had friends who were not able to raise their sons as they would have wished, and that inspired in the mentor a sense of what young men need. Many are tired of seeing young men fall short of their potential, and tired of working to shoulder the burden that underachieving men place on all of us.

Most report finding it deeply rewarding, but in a way that requires patience. Kendrick Harris describes his first experience, at another school before Eagle, this way: "My first match started to frustrate me. I remember going to his social worker and saying, 'I don't know if I can go on much longer. It's not really working out personality-wise. I don't think I'm influencing the kid.' The social worker gave me such crucial advice. He said, 'This is the deal. You are going to have to accept that you may not see—most likely will not see—all of the effort you're putting in with this young man come to fruition. You're going to have to do this thing with the belief and the understanding that at some point it's going to click, it's going to affect him, but you may not be there when it happens.' Since then, I've had mentees come back to me, sometimes years later, kids who never seemed to open up to me, and say, 'Thank you so much. You don't know what you've done for me.'"

Reflecting further on his years of mentoring for several organizations, Kendrick Harris says, "I've had mentees become groomsmen at my own wedding. I've watched them go on to have careers, have their own children. That advice changed it for me. It allowed me to be the recipient of the long-term benefit of mentoring."

The surprise of mentoring is how much it can benefit the mentors. In 2012, when Eagle Academy hosted our annual Saving Our Sons conference, we had a panel discussion for educators featuring the principals of the first three Eagle schools. All three of these leaders, who function as mentors to their entire schools, from the teachers and the staff to the students and even to the parents, revealed that they themselves still have mentors to guide them forward. It's an approach to success that can guide men for their entire lives.

Mentor Jessie Wooten explains, "Every time I start a new session with a new group of young men I tell them the same thing. I thank them for allowing me the opportunity to be in their lives. I feel that I am not worthy of them, because they teach me so much. They've helped me become a better man and a better husband because they hold me accountable and they allow me to share something of myself. Maybe I'm the one who didn't have the opportunity to reveal myself, but now you're allowing me a safe haven to be vulnerable with other men, young and old. I get choked up every time I start thinking about this, because it's so important that they understand that we are here because we care. We are black men in our black communities, raising strong black men and being accountable to our communities. We are not begging for someone else to come in and do something, we're standing up ourselves, getting off the sidelines and doing something notable, not because we want to be noticed but because what we're doing is of notable stature."

CHAPTER SEVEN

"I WILL STAND UP TO YOU"

Discipline to Teach, Not Punish

Into my office came the students that most teachers would do anything to avoid. Arriving by ones and twos from their classrooms that first year in the Bronx, they looked around the room, confused. All these young men had been sent to the principal's office before—and worse. Many had a history of suspensions and other disciplinary infractions long enough to jam a printer. But why had I called them this time? And why in this group?

In came Charles Miller, the chronic fighter, and Edward Gordon with his curly hair and big dark eyes, smiling that bucktoothed smile I was never sure I could trust. Soon twenty young men were pressed into my office—the principal's office—a room meant to hold half that many. Their faces hardened as one and then another figured out what they all had in common. I'd told their teachers, "I want to have a meeting with the knuckleheads," the students who gave us the hardest time. Frequently absent or casually late, they showed up to school lethargic, lifeless, unwilling to participate—or suddenly disrespectful, fighting and wreaking havoc. The "knuckleheads" were the seemingly unteachable ones, the ones whose teachers may well have felt, *It's a wrap! This one's heading for prison and I can't do a thing for him.* Some of these young men would try to buy beer in the morning right there in the deli where I stopped to get my breakfast. Some I'd found smoking marijuana around the corner from school when they were supposed to be in class. I hadn't been used to that kind of brazen behavior when I was principal of my previous school.

These young men could make their own parents throw up their hands. *What do I do with this boy now? I'm not even sure how to raise him anymore.* Some parents would say, "He's not my little baby anymore. He was cute and huggable and loveable. Now he won't listen—and he's huge." Others said, "He's still my little baby! I can't tell him no. What do you expect me to do?" But whether a struggling parent feels like giving up or giving in, they all share a similar fear: Maybe this wayward young man isn't reachable anymore. Maybe it's too late for my son.

Now the knuckleheads crowded onto the couch and the chairs around the conference table. They filled the folding chairs brought in especially for this meeting. They were all ninth graders, but some were sixteen, even seventeen years old, big as linebackers. At least one was a gang member. One was already a father. They wore their school uniforms of shirt, tie, and slacks—I had established my authority that far—but they looked mostly at the floor or at each other, not at me. Some slouched in their chairs, legs straight out, arms crossed over their chests as if rejecting everything and everyone around them.

"I called you to my office," I told them, "because the teachers have to talk to me about you all the time and I'm sick of it. You can't go on as students here if you don't learn what it takes to be an Eagle—to be leaders, not followers. To become young men who don't run behind others and do destructive things just because others do."

I wanted them to feel they faced an important test, but the truth was that our school faced that test with them. The teachers whose classes were disrupted, who had been chronically ignored or insulted to their faces, were waiting to see whether this new school could handle young men like these. The parents who were throwing up their hands were watching to see whether our approach could get different results from what had failed them before. Already that first year, more than half of our students had grown into solid citizens who showed up for school, treated their teachers with respect, worked hard, and took good advantage of what we offered them, but although most of our students had no discipline issues, those who did drained our energies and sapped our morale. They got far more than their share of our energy and attention, which limited what we had left for the rest. I could talk as tough as I liked about the need for them to shape up, but the truth was that we would all succeed or fail together.

Now I told the students who had gathered in my office, "You have to understand that there is a difference between going to the school called Eagle Academy and *being an Eagle*. It's my hope that one day you will transform yourselves into Eagles and soar. But what I know today is that something has to give."

A room full of young men stared back at me. *Yeah? So what. So what, Mr. Banks?* They'd heard all this before. Some had been hearing a version of this speech since kindergarten. *What are you going to do about it, Mr. Banks?*

What could I do? I took out a book, a collection of photos in black and white, and opened it up on the conference table. "Take a look at these pictures," I said. The students seemed surprised, but they gathered around. I suppose it was better than being lectured again about their disappointments and failures.

The pictures reproduced in the book showed young men my students' age and a little older, brown-skinned young men, some alone, some with their families, notable for their old-fashioned clothes and the disturbing fact, which took a few moments to come clear, that they were all dead. Some were hanging from tree limbs with nooses around their necks. Many pictures showed members of the white mobs who had done the lynching or gathered to watch the killings as entertainment, sitting around, picnicking, smiling. Some of these photos had been sold as postcards.

Not so long ago, I told my students, lynchings like those pictured in this book, *Without Sanctuary,* were common in many parts of the country. "This is what some of our ancestors went through," I said. "This could have been your great-grandfather, your great-uncle, hanging from one of those trees." For me, this was a story I'd heard since childhood, but I'd learned not to assume that anyone had taught our young people their history.

None of the boys seemed lethargic now. No one was sitting back with his arms crossed and his legs stuck out straight. After they had all gotten a chance to look, I left them slowly turning pages and I went to shut off the lights. It was still afternoon, so the room didn't go fully dark, but with the lights out it felt more like a theater. I told the young men that now I wanted to show them a video clip, part of the miniseries *Roots.* I remembered it from when I was a kid and it became the most-watched program in the history of television. But when I'd mentioned it to my Eagle students, I'd found to my amazement that most of them had never heard of it.

I played them the scene where Kunta Kinte, a Mandinka tribesman cruelly taken from his family and community in Africa, refuses to accept his new life in America as a slave. When he won't answer to the new name that his slave master has chosen for him, an overseer has him whipped, brutally and at length, until his will finally breaks. He answers to his slave name.

I stopped the video and I told the students, "I want you to

try to understand the history. There were people before us who fought, bled, and died. There were survivors who were abused and maimed. Now tell me, what did they hope for? What did they dream about?"

A teacher can feel when he or she has students' attention. Right now they were locked in on what I shared with them, and were quiet and focused. I told them, "Those people would have given anything to have exactly what you have right now: the opportunity to go to school, get an education, and make a much better life for yourselves and, one day, your children."

I went on to say that while there are still inequities in America today, back in the time of slavery reading itself was illegal. Both the slave and the person who taught the slave to read were punished by the state. And after emancipation, freed slaves became some of the biggest supporters of public education for all. "The chance you guys have been given at a school like Eagle is something they could only dream about. Now tell me: How in the name of these people, your ancestors, can you *not* come to school and give your best?"

It was almost the end of the period, so I finished by saying, "The chains are off our bodies, but the chains may not be all the way off our minds. You are the ones we're counting on to turn it around. You are our hope for the future."

The bell rang, signaling the end of the period. I asked the students to carry out the extra chairs from my office. They walked out quietly. A few said, "Thank you, Mr. Banks."

Once they were gone, I sat down at my desk. I took off my glasses and rubbed my eyes. No onetime intervention would solve anything, I knew, but this first meeting with the most challenging students felt right to me. If we at Eagle could paint this picture, over time we could help these young men see who they are—their place in the histories of their communities, their sense of urgency about their studies, and their promise for their future. If they could see what their forebears had overcome, they could start to imagine themselves getting off the sidelines and back into the game. They might begin to picture the triumphs they could reach if they developed the talents they had been given and the character they would need. They might start to imagine themselves not as nobodies fated to go nowhere, but as fortunate young people full of potential, with a destiny to fulfill. They might feel they had an important mission. I thought, *We have to do more of this.*

"YOU HAVE NO IDEA"

I was still sitting there with the sounds of students' voices echoing down the hallway when I heard a crash—a tremendous impact, metal smacking into metal. Through my office door I glimpsed Natasha Steed, the school safety officer, running through the lobby, her blue uniform a blur. "I saw who did it!" she yelled. "I saw it on the security camera!" Thinking that a fight was starting, I ran out into the hallway to assist before a bigger melee developed.

But Natasha was standing by the stairwell door with one lone student—Edward, with his handsome face and his buck teeth. A chair lay on the hallway floor where he had thrown it against the metal stairwell doors. I told her, "Let me have him," and I brought him back into my office.

When I asked him what happened, he said that one of the girls from the co-ed school that shared our building had called him a name.

"So you threw a *chair* at her?" I yelled.

"Yep," he said.

"If that chair had hit her, you could have killed her!"

"She ducked," he said.

"Thank God," I said.

I looked at him, face-to-face, the two of us in my office with the door closed. I said, "You were just sitting with me here in this room.

I just talked to you about the craziness and the suffering our people have been through. And you *threw a chair* at this girl? After what we just spoke about! Are you that messed up?"

He looked at me with those big dark eyes—not confrontational, not ready to fight, but like a little boy, almost sheepish. As if to say: *I can't control it. I'm a screwed-up kid and I don't know what to do.*

"Are you *really* that messed up?" I demanded again.

He looked me dead in my face. "Yep." As if to say: *You have no idea. You have no idea how messed up I really am.*

And I remember wondering, *What do you say to that?*

CAN THIS FIGHT BE WON?

Since the founding of Eagle Academy, our message was clear. *The cavalry is here! We've come to save you guys.* But that first year, I learned that not all of our students seemed to speak our language. It was as if we had found them drowning in the Hudson River and we were throwing life preservers—only to watch these guys let them float away in the current. We might have used words like *dysfunction* when we wrote the concept paper and the grant applications for the school, but it was a different thing to look into Edward's eyes and realize this was one young man we may not be able to save.

These young men I had called to my office had been through so much, they had put on a kind of psychic armor to survive. Inside that armor, it's harder to get hurt, but it's also harder to feel anything. It's harder to hear and to see. Life inside that armor is a life in darkness, a darkness you can almost see in their eyes, as if some essential lamp inside them is being allowed to flicker and to die.

After Edward looked out at me from deep within his psychic armor, showing me that he had accepted his place in there, as if he expected to be in that darkness for the rest of his life, I felt defeated. At home that night, I told my wife, Marion, about our confrontation. She had grown up in the toughest housing project in Jersey City; now she worked in the Newark public schools. I said, "There's a reason no one else is doing this." She just nodded. No one needed to explain to her what a heavy lift it would take to make Eagle a success.

Those most difficult young men tested us again and again. Any one of them could explode at any moment, like Edward hurling that chair at a fellow student, and you only needed a couple of explosions to give you a very, very long day. But after that talk with Edward, I began to feel like a boxer who had lost his big fight. It was as if I had always relied on my right hook to get the knockout, but when the crucial moment had come and I'd thrown my best shot, it wasn't good enough. That punch might have made the other guy back up a few steps, but he was still standing. My opponent—the environment that shaped these young men's lives—was so powerful, it seemed to have damaged their souls. The work we engaged in at Eagle was harder than anything I had expected. At times, I questioned our single-sex approach. Were we right to work only with young men? Maybe, I thought, some of their emotion would get buffered if there were girls in the room. I began to worry: *Maybe the doubters and the nay-sayers are right, and this fight can't be won. Maybe we're too late to save these young men.*

It was a thought that went against everything I believed. I remember once when we were negotiating with a school principal about the possibility of Eagle sharing space in his school building while we built our own campus. He asked for a big meeting, and he brought along several members of his staff as well as many parents of his students. I brought my father. The principal told me, "We respect the work you're trying to do, we just don't want you doing it in this building. If you come here, we all know what's going to happen. All the parents are going to be trying to get their sons into your school and I'm going to be stuck with the leftovers."

"Maybe that's where you and I part ways," I told him. "I never refer to any of our kids as leftovers."

I thought I was giving him a little room to back out of an unfortunate word choice, but he wasn't interested.

"Maybe you don't," he said, "but I do."

Later my dad told me, "You know what the most damning thing was? All those parents sitting there and none of them said a word against him."

No matter where you look in education, there is a dangerous tendency to separate "good" kids from "bad," and then to write off the "bad" ones—almost always young men—as beyond saving. I can never accept that. My brother Philip might have been considered one of the "leftovers," and look how he has soared. Even "knuckleheads," the term I sometimes use for the most challenging young men, is meant as a term of endearment. But in so many inner-city schools, I find that the teachers and sometimes, as in this case, the parents and the principal, too, have mentally separated the worthwhile "good" ones from the "leftovers," the hopeless.

In many urban charter schools I have seen, they make the same division, they just slice up their student body differently: the school will teach to the girls and the more middle-class boys, and "counsel out" the inner-city boys, quietly encouraging them to leave for traditional public schools before they damage the school's graduation statistics. In public schools, boys of color are most often the ones treated as unreachable. And increasingly, schools across the country are teaching to the girls and treating the boys of all backgrounds, except for a small number of exceptionally "good" ones, as beyond saving. So many different kinds of schools with different populations, but the same story: energetic, rude, disruptive, aggressive, i.e, "boyish," behavior will get a student marked as too difficult to help, and another promising young man will be lost.

I refused to accept that there was any category of young person who was beyond help. But at the same time, I was feeling the sheer physical strain of standing up to these most troubled young men. If I was going to keep on with this work, I realized, I was going to have to dig deeper.

THE STRENGTH TO SAY NO

What can we do about young men at their most challenging and frustrating? First, whether we are parents or educators, we must stand up to them. It takes a lot of commitment and a little creativity. I remember one morning when the mother of a student called my home in a panic. Her son wouldn't go to school, she said. He wouldn't even get out of bed. My wife took the call. The student's mother told her that she didn't think she could handle her son anymore. But my wife didn't have much patience for parents who won't discipline their children—which means, first of all, disciplining ourselves. She told the student's mother, "Sure, you can handle him. Why don't you put down the phone and go fill a pitcher with water. Pour that water over your son. He'll get out of bed."

When Edward made me feel like the losing boxer in a fight, I thought to myself: *I need to get back in training.* There would be many more moments when I'd have to take angry young men into my office, so I had better be ready. I started lifting weights again, working out to build up my physical strength, not because I would ever engage one of my students physically, but because I needed for them to know, and for me to know as well, that I had the strength and the stamina to stand up to them.

When one of those young men cursed a teacher out or engaged in other rude, disrespectful, or dangerous behavior, it made my blood boil. Anyone on my staff can tell you that when I'm really provoked, I take off my glasses and rub my face, and then I get very intense. It's almost as if I transform and the young man sees a different person. I get right in his face. I look him dead in the eye. I say, "Look at me! Do I look like I'm afraid of you? What you just said to that teacher, what you just did to that other student—that is not just disrespectful of them, it is a straight diss to me." I don't denigrate them with my words, but I tell them that they will not disrespect me either.

Someone has to be the tough one who faces up to a young man. Who says, "No, you can't do that," over and over again if necessary. We have students who come to school out of uniform or with known uniform violations, testing us—*Do the rules really apply to me? Do my teachers actually care?* We send them to detention, day after day if necessary. Sometimes we have students who come to school drunk or high, and we call a family member to come in. We may send them home with instructions to come back the next day. If it happens again the next day, we make the call home again. And the next day. And the next day, if necessary, until one morning they decide to try following the rules. In the same way, if they engage in destructive behavior, someone has to be there to stand up to them, every single time. When I was principal I often had to say, "This is my house! I built this for all the young men who want to transform their lives. I'm here every day, and I will not allow you to come and desecrate what we have built here." Sometimes I acted a little carried away—a little more carried away than I felt—in order to make an impression.

After an encounter like that, it's important that the young man have a chance to talk about what has happened. Their counselor will reassure them that what appeared as an act of aggression on my part, or on a dean's part, was really an act of compassion and concern.

THE SAME RULES FOR EVERYONE

The most important thing I can say about this approach to discipline is that there are not a different set of rules for different sorts of young men. It's the same rules, the same approach we use with every young man, only we apply them more firmly and louder for those who need it underlined. It is still a matter of high expectations, security, and love. I may have to take a hard line with a student and tell him that we will not tolerate his falling below our expectations in how he treats his teachers, his fellow students, his school, or himself, but at the same time I am offering him security. I am saying, *You're safe here. I won't let you destroy this place. I won't let you destroy yourself.* It's a form of safe passage through the most dangerous parts of themselves. By standing up to them I'm saying, *I'm here with you and I will protect you.* I show them my strength and my seriousness so they can understand: *Mr. Banks can handle me. I am not a terror that no one can contain. He's got me.*

How do they respond? Some start crying. Many have never had a grown man speak to them in this way. Some have had to play the role of man of the house prematurely, because there was no one else to do it. Now, confronted by an actual man, a strong man, a responsible man who does care, a lot of pent-up emotion can come pouring out, not about our conflict mainly, but about their own lives.

Aaron Barnette, the dean of students in the Bronx, explains, "Everything I do is out of love. I spend more time at Eagle than I do at my own home. I love these guys and I have no problem telling them that, even when I'm yelling and getting on them. So while they might not say it to me, I'm sure a lot of them feel: *Wow. That's what it feels like to have a father who cares enough to yell.*"

When I have to take a hard line with a student, and then I see him exiting school at the end of the day, I will pull him aside, put my arms around him, and tell him, "I want you to have a great day. Think about what we talked about earlier and tomorrow let's make a fresh start. I'll see you in the morning when you come in. And remember I care about you. I want the best for you. So are we good? Have you got it?" These kids crave that kind of strong but not abusive presence. When I see them the next morning, I give them a big firm handshake, a slap on the back, and then I look for the first opportunity I can find to acknowledge them at a town hall meeting for something good they've done.

For some young men, that's enough. They need to hear that strong voice and those consistent rules and regulations, and then they will open up to the opportunities we can give them. They realize they are in a good place, a safe place, where we're not going to let anything terrible happen to them, and they can take the armor off. It's a relief for them to discover a place where they don't have to be the tough guys. They can just be little boys, grow up nicely, have fun, learn, work hard, and have a great life.

Who doesn't want that? In my experience, every child yearns for that, particularly those coming from a life full of chaos and fear. Who wouldn't want to attend a school—or come home to a family—with stability, strong leadership, and a welcoming culture, where you can feel safe? Your whole soul wants it.

No one wants to be a tough guy. That's just an attempt to protect ourselves from bad experiences we have had. Given our druthers, we'd all have been nice corny kids. For that reason, I tell people that the work we do with young men, even the most challenging young men, is not revolutionary. Underneath their armor, the toughest young men have the same hopes, needs, and desires as anyone else.

WHAT DISCIPLINE MEANS

A young man's need for a father figure, someone not necessarily big but emotionally strong, someone to stand up to him and guide him, seems to go even deeper than psychology. It's part of our biology. In the *60 Minutes* episode "The Delinquents," which so many of our Eagle mentors watch and refer to in their work, a national park in South Africa sets out to solve a mystery: someone is brutally killing the rhinos in the park. The killers are not poachers, however, as the park rangers can tell because the dead rhinos are found with their horns still intact on their heads. The rangers slowly discover that the rhinos are being killed by young male elephants, some of whom are also attacking safari buses filled with tourists. But that still leaves a mystery: Why?

An investigation reveals that the young male elephants that were running wild had been transferred as juveniles from a different national park after their parents were killed. These traumatized, orphaned elephants then became unsupervised adolescents. Lacking adults to teach them to behave, they began to commit violence. The solution? The park moved grown male elephants to live near the rampaging adolescents, and the grown males stood up to them and calmed them. The violent attacks stopped.

At Eagle Academy, our male authority figures and also our mentors play the role of those grown elephants, helping to reinforce the sense of a strong, caring male presence for those young men who may not have enough of it in their lives. In this way, our mentors are crucial to creating a disciplined environment. Mentor Kendrick Harris explains, "I'm kind of boisterous with the kids. I come in like I'm the poppa elephant, roughing you up a little, in your face, talking to you close. When we first meet I may grab you in a loving, caring way. I'll move you around a little bit. I'll hug you rough. So you get a sense that I'm not the one to test—but at the same time it's a loving grab."

Eagle mentor Myron Williams says, "A big part of your credibility with the young men is how you handle yourself physically. They need to understand that you can discipline them. You can help them and you can hurt them. They have to see that they can't pull your puppet strings, like they may do with their moms or their moms' boyfriends. I've been in the gym with them in morning when we're doing the warm-ups, and I'll line a few young men up on a wall. I'll say, 'If I see you move, I'm coming at you.' Then they realize: 'Oh wow, this guy's not a joke.' Not that you have to do that a lot. Just every once in a while."

I want to reiterate: I don't endorse any sort of hitting or corporal punishment. I'm talking instead about the psychological influence on a young man when he feels every day that he stands in the shadow of powerful, grown, caring men who will hold him accountable. That's a resource that more parents and educators need to recognize. We are wrong when we imagine we must choose between the corporal discipline that many in the older generation knew and the shoulder-shrugging approach more common today. We can stand up to our young men, and *you* can stand up to our young men, as I've described, showing them the way with consistent rules, clear consequences, and strong voices dedicated to their well-being.

Here is what we have learned at Eagle Academy. If a young man believes he is on a promising path, with strong role models who will stick by him—in part because he's had the chance to test them, and test them again, to prove to himself that they believe in him, even when he goes wrong—then he's not going to walk around with his underpants showing. He's not going to disrupt his classroom until he makes his teacher's life a living hell. He's not going to hit someone up-side the head and take her purse. He's not going to rampage through the neighborhood spreading misery. Those are the behaviors of people who see nothing positive ahead of them, who are trapped in their own armor and living in darkness, who believe they will always be left alone in the darkness. But those who can see a light up ahead, even if they haven't reached it yet, and who feel that others travel alongside them, committed to their journey, can achieve extraordinary things.

The challenge, of course, is when a kid like Edward Gordon, who has done something outrageous, listens to you talk, seems to understand what you are saying—and then two days later he does it again. What we have found at Eagle is that when we can be consis-tent, slowly the message will get through to most of them. That first year with the so-called knuckleheads, we went from twenty kids who were profoundly challenging down to ten. Ultimately, we got down to five. Along the way, we realized that some needed a much greater degree of help and support than any school official or teacher or parent can give—that's when you turn to a social worker or psychologist, referring the young man and perhaps the whole family for outside counseling.

But even after we have helped them to find outside help, there are further approaches we can continue to take for those young men who are still trapped in their own armor and their cycle of destructive behaviors.

EVERY INCIDENT IS AN OPPORTUNITY

Every serious incident has to be addressed on its own terms, but very often it is also a moment when the young man committing the infractions is asking certain questions: *Is anyone out there listening? Can anyone handle the problems that make me want to explode? Am I bound to fail?* The day Edward threw his chair at a fellow student and showed me he had accepted his lot in life as a failure and a future criminal, I didn't know what to say. But in time I realized he was not delivering a final verdict. He was asking for help. What I needed to be able to say, to him and to any young man who seems to be writing himself off, was this: "I don't accept your failure. You may have no one in your life who can stand up to you, but I will stand up to you. I don't believe this is your fate. You don't have to give up on yourself."

EVERYDAY MANHOOD

If every crisis is a chance to break through to a young man trapped in emotional armor, there are other opportunities, quieter ones, every day, to show young men a better alternative. The word *discipline* comes from the same root as the word *disciple*. It doesn't mean to punish with pain. It means to teach. Jesus taught his disciples how

God expected them to live. When we have a discipline issue with a young man, we should be teaching that young man what his school, his family, and his community expect of his behavior—that is, how to live better.

One of the clearest ways we do that is in our choice of where and by whom discipline is enforced. Principal Rashad Meade of our Brooklyn campus says, "It's important to me not to outsource discipline. It is extremely rare that I suspend students out of school. They all need to know that I'm not going to get rid of them for a number of days or send them away to another school altogether. I might give a student an in-school suspension, but I'm not going to send him to sit at home, with no one to help him understand the effects of his infraction on his community."

It's more valuable in the long run, for everyone, if we keep the student where we can talk to him. Sometimes as a principal I ask a student who's been sent to my office to calculate how many hours of his education he would miss if he got suspended again. I ask him to think about the class notes and homework assignments piling up while he's gone, and how much work he'll be doing to make it all up, even after the suspension is over. At the end of a conversation like that, I might offer him a chance to make amends for his infraction by doing something for the school, such as cleaning the desks, rather than having a formal suspension. (I include the parents in those conversations, and never once has a parent said, "No! Suspend him!") The point is to make sure that even in the way we discipline young men, we bring them closer. When they internalize that, it reinforces the feelings of respect, family, and brotherhood.

When we keep a young man close, even when his behavior has been unacceptable, we can try to help him see himself and his choices in the future. Part of detention at Eagle Academy is the conversation we can have about being in detention: *How did you get here? What's your side of the story? All right, well, the next time that story starts up in your life, what could you do differently?* But to help him see his possibilities differently, we have to be open to seeing the student differently. It's easy for adults to throw up our hands and say, "How could you do these things? You must be crazy!" It's more work to say, even to myself: Here we have Charles Miller, full of anger after his mother left the family. His big beef with the world was that he was the little guy. So how does a small, quiet, angry boy establish himself in the South Bronx? He fights. Charles would stand his ground—it didn't matter how big his opponent was. He'd take on any challenger. And other kids got to know that about him, to realize how thin-skinned he was, and they'd push his buttons to get a reaction and watch the fight.

We could easily have seen Charles as a terror, one of the most aggressive, troublesome young men ever to come through Eagle's doors, something to fear and push away. But we had the choice to see him instead as a small, insecure kid with a great spirit, a great resiliency, who was using his strength and determination in all the wrong ways, but who had the capability of using them differently. Once we could see that possibility, then each time he was sent to detention or to my office, we could start talking to him about alternatives. I would ask him, "How many times are you going to do this? How many times do you think you'll get hit hard in the head? That can't be so easy on your brain. Is that really how you want to use the brain God gave you?"

It takes a lot of talk. I go over these lessons constantly with young men. Sometimes I can see the reaction on the kids' faces: *"Not again . . ."* I probably would have felt the same way, getting a talk like that when I was teenager. But those are talks they remember, and they remember not just what I said to do or even why I said to do it, but the story behind it, the reasoning and the meaning of the story. That's something a man can carry with him his entire life.

One of the most convincing ways to show a young man the depth of our caring is through our actions. Dean of Students Aaron Barnette tells this story about a time he realized that Charles Miller was about to get into yet another fight, one of the most dangerous of his life. "One day after school he was outside with a group of his friends. With my job I need a nose for trouble brewing, and that day drama was in the air.

"I came outside and I saw Charles at the end of the block with a whole bunch of his friends. Up the block there is another group of guys, a very large group. This was at Eagle's old building, and it was in a heavy gang neighborhood. The other group is pointing at Charles, saying things. Charles is doing some serious tough-guy posturing.

"I said, 'Charles, what's going on? The school day is over.'

" 'Nothing. Nothing's wrong.'

"By this point I could see that the guys up the block were coming for him. There were a whole lot more of them than there were of Charles and his friends.

"I said, 'Come into the school.'

" 'No, I'm not coming.'

" 'Charles,' I said. 'Come into the school now.'

"I literally had to grab him and force him in the doors of the school, with him fighting to get away from me, the dean who was always spoiling things, always getting in the middle of things. But he sent me a message on Facebook later. It said: *I could go on for days about how your words and advice helped me through life without you even knowing it. The day you physically brought me back into the school, people were looking for me. You saved my life. . . . Thanks for seeing your job as more than a job or career. Thanks for making it a mission. And most of all: thanks for not aborting the mission. I can't imagine a me today without your presence throughout my life.*'"

Whatever a young man is doing that gets him in trouble, we don't just stand up to him to stop the bad behavior. We try to talk to him about what's at stake in the choice he made to get into that behavior. For a student who lies to teachers or cheats on his work—someone who doesn't commit violence, but tries to "get over" on people, like my old friend Robert who cheated the rest of us boys out of our marbles—we talk about character. *Who are you, deep down? Who are you when no one else is looking? Do you really want to be the guy bringing the Zion marbles to cheat all of his friends? Aren't you better than that?*

If you get your education and you're not going to be one of the good guys, then who needs you? Bernie Madoff was a highly educated man, with the skill set to be one of the most successful people in the country. But he was the one with the Zion marbles, the guy who wanted to get over. He hurt so many people in a way that went far beyond the guy who knocks someone over the head. He took their life savings. *Don't be that kind of guy!*

That's what we say at Eagle, and we're always saying it. A constant beating of the drum: *Don't go that way, guys! There's a better way over here, a much better way.*

THE VOICES OF HIS BROTHERS

Sometimes the people who are most effective at getting through to a young man in the darkness are the peers he trusts. When I see the opportunity, I will lay out an incident to a small group of a young man's peers, ones I know he respects, listens to, and doesn't want to disappoint. I say something like, "This young man in front of you was caught doing X. I spoke to him about it and this is how he responded to me. What do you think?" Then I'll give the students fifteen minutes to talk to him while I observe from a distance. It's almost like peer tutoring, with the subject being right and wrong action. As with tutoring, the young men themselves often have their own uniquely direct way of explaining the situation—and a degree of authority with their peers that it's hard for an adult to equal.

When I was the principal, Eli Moran, a former member of the Latin Kings gang, was one of the best students I knew at supporting our disciplinary efforts with positive peer pressure. Even after he quit the gang, he still had a tough edge. People knew not to mess with him, though he was now walking around with a smile and a whole different spirit. A lot of guys were still scared of Eli and I used that to my benefit. I could pull Eli aside and tell him, "I need you. The teachers have spoken to this kid but now we need you to help him understand what it really means to be an Eagle. Only you can help me now." A natural leader, he reveled in his new role as elder statesman. I'd bring him in to talk to a kid who was behaving as he had behaved in the past, and he would say, "Don't be like that—that's how I was, and look at me now. I'm doing so much more now, and my life is so much better." Several of our graduates today credit Eli with keeping them in school.

RULES THAT TEACH

The test for any method of discipline is ultimately what it teaches. Even rules should teach. At Eagle we have strict rules about the use of disrespectful language toward teachers and toward fellow students. This is because our young men who get into fights often do so after they have felt that someone spoke to them disrespectfully. I can't count the number of fights that began with someone saying, "Suck my ——," or "joking" while leveling words such as *gay* or *homo,* or insulting other students' mothers. For the same reason, horseplay such as slapping the back of another boy's head or grabbing him in a wrestling hold are grounds for a serious conversation: what one student may see as playful teasing can feel insulting to another, leading to a fight. The rules are intended to prevent situations in which fights start, and to help our students develop their own awareness of their role in creating conflict. Often new students are surprised at how strict we are. As one new sixth grader put it, "Eagle is different because I always used to fool around in other schools. Here, I would have been in deep trouble."

But as strict as we are, when our students break these rules, we don't respond with outrage. Dean Aaron Barnette explains: "I'm not necessarily mad at them when they do that. I'm disappointed, and it's cause for consequences or a conversation, but I always remember that as young men of color, their only examples may be what's out in the streets. At a lot of the schools these kids have gone to, I don't know if they've even been told that they are intelligent. I don't know if they've been told it's not acceptable to sleep in class. I don't know if they've been told that you need to challenge your teachers to educate you. Our students have been schooled in behaviors that endanger their success as students, and they have missed out on learning the behaviors of successful students. The underlying point of our rules is not to catch them using "bad language" or "bad behavior" and punish them for their infractions, but to show them how accomplished scholars and citizens speak and act with one another, and reinforce those more positive habits.

SUPPORT THEM TO SUCCEED

In the same way that we provide extra study time, conferences with teachers, peer tutors, and other resources to support our young men in living up to our high expectations of their work as scholars, we must provide an equal level of *emotional* support to help them meet our high expectations of their behavior. For that reason, we are constantly on the lookout for signs of young men under more pressure than they can handle. In the mornings, there is always an Eagle staff member waiting to greet the students as they come in. When it was me, I offered each young man some lightweight banter or a little light tap on the head. I tap their heads a lot, give them a hug, to show them they are dear to me. There are so many boys who otherwise don't get that. Even if you don't have verbal contact with them, that morning contact resonates with them.

A morning greeting makes them feel welcome, but the second and equally important purpose is for someone who knows and cares about each young man to get a look at him before the day begins. Principal Meade often welcomes the young men at Eagle Academy in Brooklyn. He greets each one, and he expects to hear them respond, at least with, "Good morning, Mr. Meade!" A nod is not enough. It's never all right to let someone slide by you. As Yvette Crespo explains: "If you see a young man come in and he won't talk to you, won't say hello the way he usually does, and you don't stop him at the door, you might miss a kid on the edge. But when you stop that student and talk to him, when you look him in the eye, you can ask, 'What's going on?' We can't know what he went through last night, or what he saw at home or on the way to school. You can't let him walk by because if you do, you won't know what he's dealing with. You don't know what he might do to himself. You have to stop them and talk to them. Otherwise, another student might throw a little paper ball at him and suddenly he will explode."

If he says, "I don't want to talk about it," then you have to say, "Do me a favor, sit here for a minute."

He'll probably say, "No, I'm all right."

"I know you're all right, but I need you to sit for a minute."

At that point you have to know the individual young man you're talking with. Who does he feel most connected to? You have to go get someone in the school whom he trusts, someone he'll talk with.

And when that student comes in another morning on time, looks you in the eye, says hello, you keep offering him something positive. Like a daily mantra: "I'm still here to help you. I'm still here to help you." You slip behind him and say, "I'm proud of you, coming on time three days in a row." Or, "Your teacher tells me you're working harder than ever." Those things make a difference but you have to be consistent. The more damaged the boy is, the more intentional you have to be, more consistent. It helps to identify someone on your team—a teacher, a reading specialist, the security guard—who can perform a similar role.

BE A STABILIZER

Dean Barnette also emphasizes the ways that students rely on his physical presence in the school. Just by being in the building, he helps to keep students on the right path, rather than merely to catch the ones who have wandered off it. "I despise being away from the school," he says, "because I feel like I'm a big contributor to their rhythm. If I'm not in the building, kids want to get loose. They may take their ties off. They may drag their feet to class. I come back and I see those changes. But when I'm there, I'm a stabilizer." I had similar experiences when I was the principal. Our young men are looking for older men to share the power of their consistency, their presence, their visibility.

Over time, the behaviors we want to encourage become habits, and our absence doesn't shake their confidence. But until that happens, it's up to us to be present as the physical reminders some young men need. It's one of the reasons that when I was growing up, my parents tried to make our house a place where their kids' friends would gather. They wanted to keep us close, so their presence would remind us to make positive choices. They understood that until we were old enough and experienced enough to make those choices on our own, it was their responsibility to be the stabilizers.

CATCH THEM DOING RIGHT

Schools, like parents, can get so used to looking out for and identifying kids who are acting badly that they ignore those doing well. In most schools, the child with his name on the blackboard is the one who has acted out. If you don't create any problems, you have an anonymous life. Nobody calls your name when you're good. So we try to be intentional about recognizing young men doing the right thing. We do have special breakfast gatherings, lunchtime pizza parties, and ice cream parties to celebrate kids who are doing well—not just those at the top of the class, but the students who are recognized as model citizens overall, working hard and conducting themselves admirably. I'm often amazed at how much this corny sort of recognition means to kids. But when I think about it, I realize it still means a lot to us as adults. When people thank you publically, when they stand up and mention the good you have done, even for a small thing in front of a small crowd, it gives you a rush of good feeling.

WHAT IF IT'S TOO LATE?

I would like to say that in time we got through to Edward Gordon, the chair-throwing young man with the drug-dealing older brother, that although he seemed to accept the wreck of his life and I couldn't show him an alternative, a day came when we were able to help him make a different choice. But I can't say that. As my father has often reminded me, even our best efforts only improve the odds. We can't save every young man.

What we can do, and what we have done, is improve our approach for the ones it's not too late to help. The hard truth we discovered that first year at Eagle is that ninth grade is simply too late to get through to some young men. And we learned something from that: we can't wait until ninth grade. When we opened our second Eagle school, in Brooklyn, we started with a middle school. Now all the Eagle schools are designed to go from sixth through twelfth grade. Sixth graders, no matter what they have been through, don't have the same armor as ninth graders. That makes our job easier, and gives us more time to complete it.

I want to end this chapter with a little more about Charles Miller, who was as difficult as any young man we've had at Eagle, but who benefited from all of the approaches I've been describing. As you'll remember, Charles disrupted Ms. Chiluiza's class and started countless fights, served some time in juvenile detention, then returned to school and went right back to fighting. The difference was that now he seemed to be the one in charge. He had learned to manipulate other young men into fighting on his terms, and he was winning many more of his fights. We tried to reach him with a mentor, but he would not trust the man, and soon stopped meeting with him. He did however, admire our basketball coach. He had even tried out for the team during freshman year, but he didn't make it. Coach Rodney Plummer saw a lot of his younger self in Charles—they were both short, about five foot seven; both children of single-parent families; and both chronic fighters as teenagers. After hearing about yet another of Charles's fistfights, Dean Barnette approached Coach Plummer and asked him to try to get through to Charles. The coach had one of those moments of insight that makes mentoring work: *I know what that person is going through, because I went through it myself. I might be able to show him how to get where he's going. I just might be the guide he's looking for.*

The coach took Charles aside. This was no ordinary bit of mentoring, though. This was a disciplinary intervention. As he tells it, "I put my finger in his face and said, 'I'm sick and tired of hearing about you fighting with other Eagles, so this is the deal. You're on the basketball team now. Starting today, you better come to practice, you better be in uniform, and you better get there on time. Don't make me come find you. And if playing and working out with the team doesn't take all of your energy, I'll fight you myself.'"

Charles was shocked, but he showed up for practice. Quickly it became clear that he was no athlete. He loved basketball and he played aggressively, but he was not good enough to compete on the court. He said, "Coach, I can't do this. I really don't play ball. I don't want to play."

Even so, Coach Plummer saw how Charles commanded attention. The other students listened when he spoke. So the coach made him the manager, responsible for traveling with the team, taking care of the equipment, and speaking for the coach when he was away. His new role started to affect his behavior and we all noticed the changes. He was not so combative. He took responsibility for the team. He kept the players on the team focused. Coach Plummer helped him discover that he had leadership skills, that he was not just a fighter but also a fine negotiator and tactician, and in this way he started an ongoing conversation with Charles about recognizing the young man's skills other than fighting, and how he might make different use of them.

As they spent more time together, Coach Plummer always made sure to talk with Charles about more than basketball. One day he told Charles about his headaches. When he was young, he said, he would wake up every morning with a splitting headache. His head hurt so badly because he was tensing his facial muscles all day to maintain his intimidating look, part of his tough-guy persona. The coach saw Charles doing the same thing, and told him that it wasn't necessary. He already commanded respect, the coach said, so he didn't need to wear a permanent scowl anymore. And one day Charles came to school without the scowl. That day, a piece of the armor had come off. For the first time, we could see his natural face.

What is the crucial moment when a young man breaks out of his own emotional armor? There is no single moment. It is a series of changes, spread over different places and occurring with different people, so that no one, not even the young man himself, can ever account for all of it. Charles says now, about his scowl, "It's one of the things I can't ever really fix completely. But I try to smile more." No one on the outside can remove the armor. Only the person inside has that power. But someone trusted can encourage and assist, as Coach Plummer did for Charles Miller, helping him take off one piece, then another.

When the young man hidden underneath begins to emerge, and that light is shining freely again, anyone can see the change. Yvette Crespo says, "One day you realize that the light has gone on. It happens at different times for everyone. Then you can see—he got it! And *he* got it! And wow, even *he* got it! *You* remember all that time you poured into them, all the heart and soul you poured into them, and you see that they finally got it. It makes your heart pump double."

I don't know many things more beautiful than to watch the transformation of a kid you knew to be on the wrong path, a hardened kind of kid. You realize: This is what they were born to be. They were only hardened by circumstance—but now you get past that outer shell and they are beautiful young men. You can see what they were meant to be all along.

CHAPTER EIGHT

SOAR

Scholars Who Excel, Citizens with High Character, Professionals Who Succeed

When we talk about success for young men, I believe we mean three different kinds of success, and our dearest hope is for them to develop as examples of all three: scholars who excel in learning, citizens with high character, and professionals who succeed in their careers. Success in each of these ways requires developing a different aspect of a young man's identity, and it grows slowly, with guidance. When we guide young men to achieve all three, then we help to nurture not just good students, but people who can use their education to change their lives and their communities.

At an Eagle school, one person well positioned to see both where a young man stands today and how he might achieve all three kinds of success is the college counselor. Our first college counselor at Eagle Academy in the Bronx, Donald Ruff, was born and raised in Harlem. Mr. Ruff was known for the dreadlocks he wore with his suit and tie, and for getting students of color into selective colleges all across the country.

I'm thinking now of a day when Mr. Ruff was not getting the response he wanted from his students. He had sent an email to the senior class: "Great news!" he wrote. "Eagle students are eligible to apply for eight college scholarships, each one worth eight thousand dollars." He attached the application and then he waited for their response. He got nothing. Not a single student filled out the application. No one even replied to his email. What was going wrong? Couldn't anyone at Eagle use eight thousand dollars toward tuition? Didn't our students care about their futures?

A COLLEGE-GOING CULTURE

Our students and their parents cared about education, but most had not yet fully developed what we call a culture of college. Yes, many students aspired to go. Many had dedicated themselves to academic success and to building up their "brag sheet" of extracurricular activities. But they did not yet see their identities as Eagle scholars extending beyond high school graduation. They didn't think of themselves as committed to a multiyear journey in which, among other things, they would have to master the ins and outs of college costs and financial aid.

The dangers of an incomplete scholar-identity were something Mr. Ruff understood from personal experience. Growing up in a housing project in Harlem, the child of a single mother, he received a scholarship to an elite and competitive New York City independent school but resisted going. "A lot of young people don't know what's best for them," he explains. "My mother put me in a scholarship program when I didn't want to do it. Then I received a scholarship, but I didn't want it. My mother broke down crying, telling me, 'I can't afford it otherwise. You don't know what you're going to throw away!' " He attended the private school and in time was accepted to Oberlin College.

Drawing on that experience, Mr. Ruff took a risk with the new seniors who seemed to have no interest in a pool of scholarship money totaling sixty-four thousand dollars. He sent a second email to the senior class, this one copied to their parents. "There's laziness," he wrote, "and then there's pure stupidity. Not applying for money that's waiting there for you is stupidity."

Ruff waited nervously for the replies, and soon he had more than twenty. He was expecting to incur the wrath of insulted parents, but what he read was just the opposite.

"You go, Mr. Ruff!" parents told him.

"Thank you!"

"This was a message that needed to be sent."

Soon he had scholarship applications from fifteen Eagle students. That was one more step in the development of what we call the college-going culture.

TIMING

The most important aspect of winning acceptance to college may be timing. As Mr. Ruff says, "I don't just focus on the senior class—by then it's too late." That's why, on the first day of school in the first year of Eagle Academy, we held our opening day ceremony at Columbia University with the theme "Starting at the Finish Line." We offer that same message to every new class during the Summer Bridge program, in which we make a college visit as a group. Even more than girls, boys may need to have a direct experience of something before it becomes real to them. For all the conversations and admonitions about the importance of going to college, it is often not meaningful to boys until they see it for themselves. They need to walk through the student center, smell the lawn, visit a dorm and sit on somebody's bed, to understand fully that college is a physical place they can reach if they work hard enough.

In the same way, many young men need to be convinced that going to college has a point. To those raised with the expectations of attending college and ultimately having a career, it may seem obvious, but we don't make any assumptions. We explain that although there are multiple paths to success in this country, the most direct is still to get a bachelor of arts or bachelor of science degree from a four-year college. To get a degree, you have to get into college. To get in, you need good grades and a list of extracurricular experiences that display intellectual curiosity and proof of good citizenship in your community. To demonstrate those things, you have to start early and apply yourself consistently. That means by ninth grade, if not sooner, there is an advantage for those who have already identified themselves as college-bound scholars.

To start our young men imagining themselves there, we visit a college first thing, during Summer Bridge. We walk the students through the campus and sit in a lecture hall. They get the formal tour, the introductory talk from the admissions department, a talk on financial aid, and a chance to meet with young men of similar backgrounds who are students at the school. We always ask the college students we meet to speak about what they would have done differently in high school, had anyone told them what college was really like. In this way our Eagle students begin with the end in mind.

BUILD FROM DREAMS

Leaving young men feeling inspired is never enough. Just as our teachers do in the classroom, our college counselors and mentors need to show our students the nature of the college-application process, and the practical reasons it will matter in their lives. We start with their own dreams. In Summer Bridge we always take time to sit with groups of young men and ask them what they want to become when they are men. Large numbers always tell us they want to play basketball in the NBA or become hip-hop artists. Then we go to the whiteboard and show them the odds of becoming a professional ballplayer.

We draw a large box at the bottom of the whiteboard, and write in it the number of high school students playing basketball: 800,000. Above that box, we draw a smaller one, to show the number of students playing college ball: 100,000. Our students already know that there are two rounds of the NBA draft, during which 60 new players a year are selected. Then we ask them, if only 60 out of 800,000 are going to make it, what are the odds that you will play in the NBA? It doesn't mean one of them won't do it, but with those odds they have a better chance of winning the lottery. It's not a plan for buying your own home or raising a family. They need a more reliable plan, because it's likely that the NBA won't work out.

Once we plant the idea that playing ball or performing hip-hop are not reliable career choices, we start looking at the many careers related to those activities. If you go out for basketball, for example, and blow out your knee or find that you are not talented enough, you can still make money around the sport. You can report about it, coach it, become an agent, become a trainer, or work in sports medicine. Kids don't know what they don't know, so we work to show them careers related to their passions. We want to broaden their thinking beyond the stars they see on television, and get them thinking about the probability of making money from their talents and passions. That process of discovery doesn't end with Summer Bridge. Throughout the year, we have guest speakers from a range of professions who make presentations to our students, so they can learn more of the possibilities that could be out there. And this conversation that begins in summer is something that can continue with a young person's peers, parents, teachers, and mentors.

We suggest other aspirations and then work backward from those career goals to the skills they will need to build in college and in high school. Is a young man a fan of ESPN? Would he like to be a sports journalist? We can reverse engineer that for him—he's going to need to be a great writer, which means he'll have to be very strong in English, which means he has some homework to do. Now that young man has his own carrot to draw him forward. You don't have to push him.

But even when we ask them to think about jobs related to the activities they know and love, they are still confined to a very small range of possibilities. High school students tend not to know much about the varieties of work. They are dependent on the adults in their lives to help them discover what kinds of work are out there. Tiger Woods would never have become Tiger Woods if his father hadn't given him the chance to learn golf. Quantitative analysts at investment banks would never have found their careers if someone hadn't said to them: *You love math? Do you know what you can do with that?* Just as, when we host college fairs, we have representatives from sixty colleges in the cafeteria and the gym, we also host representatives from fifty-plus businesses in the classrooms, from JP Morgan Chase to Bloomberg to Google. We also provide an ongoing guest speaker series, during which our visitors talk about their careers to make students aware of what they may never have encountered before. Young men benefit when there is a real person in the room to answer questions. ("What does it mean, you're an architect? How does someone get to do that?")

THE RIGHT CAREER

How much direction do we give? I didn't tell my own kids what they should ultimately do with their lives, and I don't tell our students what careers they should pursue. I do tell them, in every way I can, to get out there and start learning what might suit them. With the students, the danger is that they won't see the point of all that effort. With the parents, the risk is that they will see our young men looking so nice in their uniforms and think we perform miracles. We don't. Our message to them about college applications is a continuation of the message they've been hearing since they were first admitted to Eagle: you have come to a place of extraordinary opportunity, but you will have to take the responsibility of activating those opportunities.

EXPLAIN WHAT IT TAKES

Once our young men see the point of college, we can explain to those who don't already know what it will take. Of course they've heard all their lives that they ought to get good grades, but what use are good grades, really, when it comes to college? One part of that answer: "Your grade point average is like a kind of money. The higher your GPA, the better chance you have to win scholarships so your family can afford to send you to college. Anything that lowers your GPA takes money out of your pocket. So if you sit in the back of the class horsing around and you miss the material you need for a test, then you just allowed the kid you were horsing around with to take your money. Are you going to let that happen?"

At the same time that we are helping our students understand the practical reasons why their grades are essential to their futures, we also have to show them that grades alone are not enough. Colleges are looking for students with demonstrated intellectual curiosity and constructive involvement with their communities. Demonstrating this takes time, in ways that both students and parents need to understand.

College counselor Donald Ruff explains, "I'm the villain. I take total control of young men's out-of-school time. It's not acceptable for them to sit at home watching television and tweeting. At the same time, as I tell parents, 'Unless your son has to work a job to help pay your rent and put groceries in your kitchen, then your son should not be working.' Our students have the rest of their lives to work for a living. While they are in high school, they need to focus on academic programs on college campuses, internships, community service, and travel abroad. That's what the students at the elite private schools and the wealthy suburban public schools are doing to build up their brag sheets, and your son will be competing against them. And I can tell you, so many times at the bottom of a college acceptance letter it says something like, 'I loved hearing about your trip to Thailand.'"

How do our kids get to Thailand or Ghana or all the other destinations to which they travel? How do we enrich their lives? We have worked hard at Eagle to build relationships with educational and travel institutions. We have a relationship with American Field Service that discounts travel abroad by 50 percent for our students.

Plenty can be done close to home. We expect our students to be working toward college throughout all of Eagle's hours of operation—from 8:00 a.m. to 6:00 p.m.—to discover and then to demonstrate their interests. Our final periods of the day offer chess, film club, varsity sports (basketball, wrestling). We participate in the Minimeds program for students interested in medical science. We are part of a program at the Apollo Theater Foundation to explore careers in entertainment and employ artists in residence to teach drum making or music through the ages. We participated in News Corporation's Journey to Excellence program. It's an ever-developing list of opportunities that we gather for our students and then urge them to take.

If your school does not provide families with this sort of information, parents and students can research it themselves—in fact, a lot of the information we have at Eagle is gathered by parent volunteers. Public libraries and librarians can help you find lists of resources for young people in the community and help with Internet searches. Other parents, neighbors, teachers, mentors, faith leaders, and community center directors often know about opportunities for young people in the area. Local news sources produce stories about new programs for young people as they are launched. Just as we at Eagle gather this information and share it with students at our morning meetings, any family or organization that serves youth can create a bulletin board of opportunities—it could even be the refrigerator door—and a time during the week to talk about them. What's essential is that parents make sure their sons are exposed to these possibilities, and that the young people pick some and try them out.

DUAL EDUCATION

Everything we teach the students about building their futures, we teach the parents. Every communication with the students is copied to the parents. Just as we have online tools to let parents track their son's academic progress day by day, we have online tools for assembling the college application so parents and other partners in the process can view their progress.

We bring in college representatives to talk about financial aid to demystify the process. Some parents don't realize that almost every family takes a loan to pay for college because it's a worthwhile investment. Unlike using credit to buy a new car that will lose half its value as soon as you drive it off the lot, using credit to buy a college education keeps paying dividends for the rest of the graduate's life. And paying back student loans can establish the credit rating that makes it possible to get a mortgage for a house. In these ways borrowing for college can be part of a longer-term financial plan.

At the same time, we have to make sure our parents know that there are ridiculous loans out there, particularly in terms of the interest rates they charge that significantly increase the amount to be repaid. There's no good in having your son in a college dorm if he is burdened by debt for decades after. We help educate the entire family about the long-term financial commitments of higher education.

DANGER SIGNS

We also rely on our parents, as well as teachers, mentors, and Eagle brothers, to watch for signs that our students are wandering off the scholarly path. Who is only doing the bare minimum of work in his classes? Who doesn't respond, week after week, when we announce news of internships and trips and other opportunities at town hall meetings or by email? Those are the young men who may find one day that they have missed their chance.

When we identify those young men who are derailing as scholars, we must stand up to them as firmly as we stand up to a student whose social behavior is unacceptable. In our very first class of college applicants, the students were still very rough around the edges even by the time they were seniors. There was a student who kept talking to his friends in the back of college counseling meetings even while Mr. Ruff was going over critical due dates for college applications. Mr. Ruff asked him to stop, and the student cracked a joke. So Mr. Ruff said, "Why don't we pull out your transcript? Why don't we see how on track you are?"

The student laughed, and some of his friends laughed with him. Mr. Ruff said, "Guys, please! You have to understand that he's laughing because he's uncomfortable." This was after a marking period in which a number of the seniors in this group, including the one making the jokes, had disappointing grades. Mr. Ruff went on, "I just need to understand why some of you don't care. Why just passing is okay. When I was growing up, eighty was failing. If I got a ninety, my mother asked, 'Why didn't you get a ninety-five?' Now I'm a black man with a three-year-old son, and I wake up in the middle of the night scared to death that my son might grow up to behave like you've been doing. I would hate to feel after I had put forth all of this energy that my son felt okay being mediocre."

He continued, "Any student who disrupts class is stealing from you. You need the confidence to check those individuals."

The bell rang to signal the end of class, and no one moved.

A few of the young men said, "Mr. Ruff, you're absolutely right. The next time, I'll say something."

"Guys," Mr. Ruff said. "You're seniors. At this point no teacher should have to ask you for your attention. You're holding on to a middle-school mentality. Do you think a professor in college is going to stop his lecture to ask you to pay attention?"

An approach like this could easily backfire. But by this point these students had an established relationship with Mr. Ruff. They saw how he came in on Saturdays for five and six hours at a time to work with them, taking time away from his own family. They knew he spoke from a place of caring—that he viewed all of them as his sons. That's part of the reason that the student he called out in class responded so well: he quit his disruptive behavior and began coming to Mr. Ruff for additional guidance. He sought out extra essay-writing workshops and other tutoring to strengthen his academic performance. He turned himself around.

But the most important benefit of Mr. Ruff's hard line may have been the discussion it sparked afterward. The other students who were known for clowning around or not giving their best started to share their reasons. One talked about a difficult home situation, and told the group what he hadn't told anyone else, that he was feeling he needed help from a therapist. Another had a mother battling cancer, which he hadn't shared with anyone at Eagle. Another was coping with applying to college when his older brother, a drug dealer, didn't approve. Because Mr. Ruff had refused to accept their self-destructive behavior as scholars, he helped free them to start addressing the deeper obstacles to the work of building their futures.

SEIZE YOUR OPPORTUNITIES

Once our future college applicants commit to their mission, we have lessons we can share with them. The first is to seize every opportunity that feels relevant to their goals. Roberto Huie, the quiet, awkward kid with the big ears whom I described in chapter three, started in right away making use of the opportunities we showed him, and he would not quit. A driven young man who wanted to make the best of himself, he was willing to step out of his comfort zone and he had the support and encouragement of a group of similarly ambitious peers. Roberto was one of the first Eagles to join a Baruch College summer program offering a college class in the morning and a leadership seminar in the afternoon. In tenth grade, he took a college survey course at Hostos Community College that qualified him to take further college courses for credit, and he began to pursue a long list of academic programs. He participated in the Fordham University STEP (Science, Technology and Engineering Program). He earned more college credits in the College Now program. Mr. Ruff used to joke, "This kid has done everything."

The summer after his junior year, he earned six college credits at Syracuse University and got a taste of undergraduate life in the dorms. But he was concerned that in a traditional college, he would be too tempted by social distractions. In an environment like that, he might not "manifest his best," as he often said.

Roberto was part of the first Eagle field trip to West Point, a busload of thirty students. Until that visit, Mr. Ruff had not considered a military academy as a place that might suit Eagle scholars. But to Roberto, West Point seemed like a way to take the Eagle Academy approach all the way to adulthood, with a guarantee of brothers and mentors to look out for him and support him as he works toward success, a worldwide fraternity that looked after its own.

He learned that the school would pay all of his expenses, meaning that he wouldn't burden his family, and he would not only fulfill his dream of entering the military like his father, he would quickly outrank him. Now Roberto's future came into sharper focus: after the trip, he told Mr. Ruff he thought West Point was the place for him.

In his years with us, he had lost his shy awkwardness and blossomed as both a scholar and as a communicator. Growing confident as a public speaker, he had shown himself to be a natural leader. His grades were among the highest in the school. Now, when classmates said that he had big ears, they often added, "like President Obama!" Roberto became our first Eagle admitted to West Point.

START EARLY, FINISH EARLY

How was Roberto able to do so much? Part of the answer is simple. He started early. When you begin building your brag sheet the summer after freshman year, you have three summers to assemble it, compared to many applicants who will only spend two summers or one. It's a head start in the race.

On the other end, there will be applicants who don't finish all their applications and those who finish in a chaotic rush. For that reason, we set our own Eagle deadlines and require our applicants to complete all of their applications ahead of the schedule given to us by the colleges. We encourage students to submit ten applications before Thanksgiving, and insist they complete all their applications before Winter Break, as opposed to the deadlines the colleges and universities set in January and later. This means they are more likely to complete their paperwork. The extra time also allows us to help parents with limited means to take advantage of the many opportunities colleges provide to get application fees waived.

To support this accelerated schedule, we have a separate class for seniors during the regular school day focused on college admissions.

In this class, we have college reps speak to seniors about what they are looking for in their applications, and Eagle graduates return from college to lead workshops on how to succeed. The students in the class support each other in the long effort of completing their applications.

IT'S NOT WHERE YOU START, IT'S WHERE YOU FINISH

Back in chapter five, I told the story of Kalim Jones, a frequently homeless young man who found a mother figure, Miss Tiddle, in church. When he came to Eagle, his connection to Miss Tiddle gave him a basis for trusting Miss Crespo, the family coordinator and unofficial Eagle mother. She in turn convinced him to give Mr. Ruff a chance, despite Kalim's distrust of men who tried to tell him what to do. Mr. Ruff guided him through the college application process, and Kalim received multiple acceptances. As he tells it: "I got the acceptance letters but I thought, 'There is no way I can afford this. There is no way I can even think about this.'"

Kalim was discovering that admission to college is not the finish line it can appear to be; it's the start of the next lap in a much longer race. Young men need support to get to college and then they need further support to continue. Each year of college has its own challenges. Parents may not understand that it's not all gravy once their son goes off to college in triumph. Scholarship money may disappear or diminish in later years. The studying gets tougher and students get lonely.

Mr. Ruff often shares the story of his freshman year in college. Although he had been a high-achieving student in high school, he didn't have the study habits he needed for college. He received failing grades and would have flunked out had he not appealed the decision with the college administration. His appeal was granted and he tried again, and then he found his way. Now when he tells that story, he also talks about Michael Jordan. Before any of us ever heard of the great basketball player, he was cut from his high school team. Setbacks like these are part of the race, even, in the case of Jordan, for the all-time greats. To get past them, young men still need the same support they have always needed.

Kalim Jones might have given up on ever being able to afford college and thrown his acceptance letters away. But he had ongoing support. "I went to talk to Ruff about paying for college and he broke it down for me. He said, 'It's a lot of money, but there are loans, there is financial aid, there are programs to apply for.' So I listened, and I was less defiant. I'd learned to value his opinion. He's someone that I really do trust."

Kalim graduated from the University at Buffalo (SUNY) with a BA in education, and took a job with Boys Hope Girls Hope as a residential counselor while he became certified to teach in New York City. He has been active in the Eagle community, serving as a volunteer tutor and pro-bono teacher assistant at the flagship school in the Bronx. He still has Miss Crespo's cell phone number memorized.

I have focused in this book on a small number of young men on the journey to establishing themselves against all odds as scholars. But there are literally hundreds of Eagle stories I could tell about every year's graduating class. Here are a few more of our early successes, to suggest something of the range of what these young men are capable of achieving, both for themselves and for the communities they help support.

- Jose Martinez, class of 2010, became Eagle's first Gates Millennium Scholarship winner. He majored in biochemistry at Hunter College and worked as a college coach for the CUNY Bridge to College summer program.
- Joe Foster, class of 2010, was drawn powerfully to the life of the streets. While growing up in a single-parent household, his older siblings were incarcerated and his younger brother died as a re-

sult of gun violence during Joe's junior year of high school. He
left Eagle for a year, but returned to complete his requirements.
As a senior his average was low, under 80, but he continues his
efforts at Pennsylvania State, where he now boasts a 3.5 GPA. He
consistently comes back to share his story with his Eagle brothers, and has served as the lead junior counselor during our Summer Bridge Program.

- Barrington Brown, class of 2009, was an academic late bloomer
  who struggled to establish his scholar-identity. He graduated
  with an associate's degree from SUNY Delhi, and was accepted
  to the Rochester Institute of Technology as a civil engineering
  tech major.

- Johns Smith, class of 2011, was raised by a single mother who
  was only minimally supportive of his life as an Eagle student.
  The family often had to live in shelters. Yet he graduated in the
  top five of his class and received the New York Urban League–
  Whitney M. Young Scholarship, among others. He made the
  Dean's List at Skidmore College with a 3.75 GPA.

- Christopher Graham, class of 2009, is a mass communications
  major (concentration in digital media) at Claflin University in
  Orangeburg, South Carolina, with a minor in theater. Host of a
  radio show, he has been featured as a public speaker at the 100
  Black Men Annual National Conference and on NBC's *Today
  Show*, and has interned at WQXR, a classical music radio station.
  He was the founding vice president of leadership for the Future
  of Success, a service organization.

- Marvin Brow, class of 2009, is a double major in juvenile justice
  and communications at Wheelock College in Boston, Massachu-
  setts. President of ALANA, the African, Latino, Asian, Native
  American Association, he served as house manager of the college's Family Theater and mentors fourth-grade boys at Matta-
  hunt Boys Academy.

- Ivan Jackson, class of 2010, attended Wheelock College as a communications and American studies major. He was president of the Black Student Union and is a student ambassador who regularly visits Eagle Academy and serves as a motivational speaker for current students.

- Jordan Liz, class of 2008, majored in economics and philosophy in the honors program at Hartwick University in Oneonta, New York, where he received the Alice Dornet Award in Economics. He began pursuing a master's degree in philosophy at the University of Memphis.

- In 2014, the first Eagle student was accepted into an Ivy League school; in fact, Brenton James was accepted by two of them.

PROFESSIONAL IDENTITY

Even at Eagle Academy, we often talk as if success in high school leads naturally to success in college and on to success in a career. But building a scholar-identity, while it is excellent preparation for a professional life, does not teach a young man to set achievable career goals. It doesn't guide his steps toward jobs that pay him for utilizing his interests, gifts, and talents.

The challenge is that when young people are starting out, their professional identities are only aspirations. A young man can say he has this interest or he wants to go into that field, but for now he has nothing to show for it. Meanwhile, there are pressures on him, sometimes intense, to show results right away. High school graduates especially need support in committing to focus on who they would like to become professionally and not just who they are right now. They need help in committing to what we sometimes call right action—making choices that will advance their lives in the direction they've chosen, which means doing what's right, not what's popular or always immediately fun. Sometimes, when students don't choose right action, it's because they are too generous, giving recklessly of themselves, such as Gerald Billups.

Gerald was the kind of young man that educators love to hold up as an example of transformation and success. He came with a discipline problem, fighting us in every sense of the word. At home, he had no father in his life. He spent a lot of time with his three sisters, and as he says, "I hated guys. I didn't want to be around guys." His fellow Eagle students picked up on his feelings about them and teased him relentlessly. Gerald had very light skin for a person of color, and other boys would tell him that his light skin was a symptom of illness. They told him he had leukemia and that he was going to die. Yvette Crespo remembers him crying every day in her office. He would come to me and demand a transfer to another school. I had to keep telling him, "The Department of Education doesn't give transfers for first-year students. If they did, they'd have ten thousand transfers a year."

Gerald kept telling us that he didn't want to be at Eagle, and we kept telling him that he was here for now so he might as well make the best of it. He had many heart-to-hearts with Ms. Crespo, even sharing his doubts about whether life was worthwhile. With her encouragement, he began to get involved in school activities. He found that involvement kept his mind off his feelings of discomfort at being around other young men. "She helped me realize there is more. There is trying to get somewhere in life. There is doing something positive."

Gerald joined the bowling team, the baseball team, and the golf program. He became part of the student body government. In time he found friends among his Eagle brothers. They not only hung out together, they studied together, and his grades improved dramatically. He participated in the New York City Police Department Explorers Program for high school students, and was chosen as one of the program's chiefs of command. Other students began looking to him as a model.

Charles Miller, who was so disruptive and prone to fights, remembers, "If you were picking on another student, he would call you out: 'Leave him alone! Why would you do that?' If a group of kids was disrupting class, he'd say, 'I'm tired of this! That's not what school is for.' He always wanted to stand out academically. He strived to do his best. And he became class president."

Gerald was selected for the Eagle Ambassador Award, given to the senior each year who best represents the Eagle ideal. He left us as a successful graduate and a model citizen with a record so clean that he could seriously pursue his ambition to work for the FBI. After graduation, he started college at John Jay College (CUNY). He was the sort of graduate any high school would be proud to showcase.

All that makes an uplifting story, but his story doesn't end there. Yvette Crespo explains, "Gerald's a giver. He'll give you his right hand and his left hand and think nothing of the fact that he's not doing for himself. He moved in with someone, a girl who came from an unstable home. He was her protector. He stopped going to college so she could go to school. I said to myself, *How could you do that?*

"She wanted to get married. She kept pressuring him to get married. I said, 'Whatever you do, trust me, no babies.' Then she got pregnant. I put on a happy face for him, but I knew a lot of things would change.

"Soon everything was about his son. He didn't think about himself. For work, he was hired as a manager at a GameStop video-game store. He thought that if he went back to school, he would be denying his son—that if he wasn't able to provide in a certain way then he was failing his son as a father. I was upset. I asked him, 'Why are you sacrificing your own life?' "

Sometimes when young men neglect their career development, it is because they are thinking short-term. When I was in college at Rutgers University, I never had money in my pocket. By contrast, I knew lots of guys back home working in stores or maybe on a clean-up crew, earning enough money to win some autonomy. It's a lot of fun to be a young man with a little money to spend, but there is a danger of outsmarting yourself. Too often, I will see a promising Eagle graduate at an event or around the neighborhood and I'll say, "I heard you're not in college. What are you doing?"

"I'm trying to put some money away first."

I understand that notion, but it's a recipe for disaster. Maybe he takes a course or two at a community college when it doesn't conflict with his work schedule. Perhaps he thinks—and his family, with little experience of college, encourages him to think—that he will get back to a four-year college "in a year or two." All too often, that's not what happens. Soon he's on a track that would require twelve years for him to finish his degree. Along the way he'll have a couple of kids, and premature fatherhood will slow him down even more.

A young man who goes that route is not a failure, certainly. He isn't an addict or an inmate. But he is a talented young man with academic qualifications who is taking the easy way in the short term and not understanding the risk to his future career opportunities.

WHEN FAMILY NEEDS YOU

When I speak to these young men who are working short-term jobs when they could be building their professional identities, they often talk to me about the people who need them. Maybe Grandma is sick and the family could use a little help. But if a young man tells me his grandma is sick, I have to ask him, "What are you, a doctor?" It's not that I don't admire the caring and good character that inspires him to do something for his family. But what he needs to do for his family is to graduate. What he needs to do for his family is to invest in himself so he has more to give them for the rest of his life.

The risk to his family, to his community, and to this country's economic future is that he gets locked into a life far below the level of his gifts and his skills. That means a young man who could have been a doctor or a corporate executive gets a job in a drugstore. He is talented and charismatic, and they promote him to manager. But that's it—he has nowhere else to go. Or he gets a job in a larger institution, but he discovers, as my father did, that there is a limit on the number of promotions you can get if you don't have a college degree. His accomplishments are limited and we all lose.

To me, the triumph of Barack Obama's election to the presidency was that a black man who had the potential to be president of the United States got the chance, for the first time in American history, to use those talents and give his best in that way for his country. When he was elected, no one knew if he would be a great president or a mediocre president, but he got the chance to give his all just like the other presidents, great and mediocre and in between, who came before him. That's my hope for every young man at Eagle, and for every young man in America: to have the chance to compete at his own natural level and to give his best. To get the same opportunity to make the most of himself that anyone else gets.

What young men need to develop their professional identities is someone to stand up for their futures. Parents, teachers, mentors, employers, investors—everyone who cares for a young man has the power to say to him, in words or by their actions, *You go out there and make the most of yourself. We'll be all right without you for a while. We'll support you as you give your all. We'll send help when the going is difficult. And we will be there waiting for you with pride and joy when you get home.*

CHARACTER AND CITIZENSHIP

My friend Kathy Cashin, a former school superintendent, used to tell her students, "I want you to be as smart as you can be, but more than that, I want you to be a good person. Because if you're not a good person, who needs you?" For young men at the beginning of their academic journey, the first test is one of character: Can they find it in themselves to become the kind of good citizens—as sons, students, peers, mentees, interns, employees—that their communities will support to achieve their best? Can they find a place for themselves?

On the other end, after the academic achievement and the launch of their professional lives, they face the test of character again. Those of us who work to support young men in their success will look to them and ask, What have they become, in their souls? Are they only out for themselves, or do they understand the debt of gratitude, the moral obligation, they owe to all the people and institutions who helped to lift them up?

I've described how Charles Miller came to us as a fighter. How he was incarcerated, came back even harder, and then he left us before he graduated, earning a high school equivalency degree instead. One day a few years later, I went to the radio station KISS-FM to give an interview, and I saw him working at the reception area. I told him how glad I was to see him, but he was very quiet, seemingly unable to talk.

As I took my seat, he whispered to his supervisor, "That's—that's my principal." The two of them looked over in my direction. I thought Charles would come chat with me, but the supervisor walked over instead. She told me what a great young man he was, how well mannered and respectful, and how much they loved having him work for the station. She said, "I don't know what's going on with him right now. He seems a little overwhelmed having you here."

Finally he came out to talk to me. He looked like a completely different kid than when he was at Eagle. At first, he could barely talk. He said, "Mr. Banks, I changed. I just want you to know, I'm not like I was."

And I said, "Oh, Charles, I'm so glad. You look great." That hardened kid so full of anger now had a completely different spirit running through him. I said, "I'm so proud of you."

"No, you don't understand," he said. "I changed." That was all he could manage to say.

In time, I learned that Charles had started college twice, but both times dropped out to take a job, in part so he could help support his daughter. Later he found work as a cook for a catering company, cooking for events at the Federal Reserve, the Barclay's Center, the U.S. Open, and various galas and auctions. He sees his daughter every day. One of his goals is to save enough to buy a two-family house, so he can rent out the bottom floor as a second source of income. He describes his life this way:

"I'm not the shiny Eagle. I didn't graduate. I went to college but I didn't finish. I had my fights, my suspensions, but they never kicked me out and I appreciated that. And now I've changed. Now I think twice. So I don't think I failed. I think I succeeded. I feel like I *have* graduated—in my thinking, my decisions, the actions I take. In my way, I am an Eagle. I even have some mentees of my own."

To me, that is the final test of character—if our young men excel but they don't give back, don't feel a deep connection to family and community, then those communities will never get lifted up. All we will have done is to provide an escape for a small number of young men, leaving those that raised them even poorer than before. We need young men not only to succeed, but to come back at least to visit and mentor the ones coming behind. We need them to be the ones who aspire in some way to be the next Barack Obama, the next Malcolm X, but also the ones who return and make Grandma proud. Otherwise, what was the point?

Success is a long road, and the young men who have the greatest chance of getting to the finish line, even when it's not on the schedule we may have imagined for them, are the ones who have character. The solid citizens. As Yvette Crespo says, "It's ideal if they go to college, but to me it's amazing that they have gotten out of the streets and turned their lives around. It's not how you start the race, it's how you finish."

SOMEONE TO STAND BESIDE THEM

Whether we are talking about success as a scholar, a professional, or a citizen, there is one factor that our successful young men talk about most: having an older person in their lives who cared about them, helped them, and believed they could rise to meet high expectations. I want to end this chapter by quoting the class of 2014 convocation speech from Eagle student Tykenji Abernathy, who describes the deepest source of a young man's success.

> We often hear the staff of Eagle talk about our legacy. What kind of legacy do we want to leave behind when we graduate? And right now the legacy I'm working on is getting rid of the boy who came into Eagle in 2010, who did nothing but fool around and almost threw his life away, and on becoming that "man" who will walk out of here in 2014 with a diploma in his hand, on his way to college. And the journey has been rough.
>
> I was that boy who was always late to class. I was that boy who never got work done. I was that boy who always got phone calls home. Like a lot of you sitting here right now, I thought I didn't need anybody. We reject a lot of the help that's offered to us. I thought I could turn in work when and how I wanted to. I also got very familiar with Dean Barnette's office. I wasn't always in his office because I liked the decorations on his walls. I wasn't always in his office be-

cause that was an opportunity to socialize with him. I wasn't always in there because the chairs were oh so comfortable. I was always in there because I did not realize that I was throwing away my chance at a successful life. I was always in there because I did not know what it meant to be a scholar. I was always in there because I did not have the motivation to do any better. And I wasn't always in his office alone.

My mother would be right there next to me for countless meetings. But these meetings were not ever for something I had achieved academically. These meetings weren't ever about how great a student I was. She was having the "his behavior" meetings. She was always having the "he's suspended again" meetings.

But there was one particular meeting that would forever change me. That one meeting between myself, my mother, and Mr. Barnette. That one meeting when I watched my mother try to fight tears, but she couldn't. I watched my mother cry right in front of me. There was a pain in her eyes like I had never seen before. What made it even worse? I was the reason. I was the one that caused my mother this pain and I cried, too.

And from that very moment, I swore that would never happen again. I swore my mother wouldn't have to come back into this building for a meeting about something I did wrong. I swore I would get my act together. I swore I would walk across that stage in June 2014 with a diploma in my hand. And I swore that the next time that I made my mother cry, that it would be tears of joy. Tears because I did something right. Everyone, and I do mean everyone, has something in their lives that will motivate them to do what needs to be done, and more. Unfortunately my motivation had to be my mother's tears. But don't let that be the case for all of you. When people tell you that you can't do something, or won't be something, don't get mad at that. Use that as your motivation. Because in 2010 I had some teachers tell me that I'd be here for five or six years if I continued on the path I was on. *But I am standing here today, with a senior tie on, getting ready to graduate on time in four years, with my class of 2014. It's never too late to get on the right path. It's only a matter of when you figure out that you are the only one that can hold you back. And the only person that can really do any damage to you is you.*

Thank you.

CHAPTER NINE

ALL HANDS ON DECK

Growing the Conspiracy of Care

In my travels around the country and even lately around the world, I get a lot of requests. Educators and politicians ask, "When are you going to build an Eagle Academy *here*?" Parents ask, "Please help my son!" The more I try to answer these two requests, the more I see that my answers, whether to a mother worried about her son or to a mayor concerned for the future of young men, are the same. First, the bad news: in most cases, we aren't coming to save the day. There are far too many places where young men or other sidelined groups would benefit from a school like Eagle Academy. We can't begin to travel to all of them and try to launch new schools. And there are far more young men whose parents would like our help than Eagle, as a single organization, could ever assist. Even in neighborhoods where we already have thriving schools, the demand for seats far outstrips the room we have in our classes. At our Queens school in 2012, with eighty spaces for new freshman, several thousand applied.

But if the bad news is no, the miracle workers aren't coming to save you, the good news is that we are not miracle workers—no more so than those asking for help. Today, when a mother comes to me and says, "It's just me and my boy. I wish we had a school like Eagle, but where we live we don't have anything like that," I will answer her, "All right, what *do* you have? Where are you starting from?"

IDENTIFY THE NEEDS

Everything we do at Eagle begins with observing the situation of the particular young men we serve. Which elements of success do they have already, and which are they missing? From the first moments we are with them, we work to create an accurate picture of our students: What physical dangers do they face? What sort of support do they have at home? Which peers do they rely on, and are those peers moving in positive directions? Can we find teachers dedicated to their success? What opportunities have they had for mentoring and for discovering the larger world of work and citizenship? Who is helping them to think about their futures, and to plan the steps, starting today, to get from here to there? As we build up our picture of these particular young men, we have two primary concerns: to help them avoid the dangers they face and to encourage them to seize opportunities to build productive and worthwhile lives.

Can I offer one standardized Eagle blueprint—the precise steps that every educator and parent should take for every young man? No. The Eagle method is based on observation: Which particular types need help? In which specific community? Because we always start with the actual young men in our care, there can never be a final version of the Eagle method. Tour different Eagle schools and you will discover that each one does things a little differently. Each one has a house system, but the ways that students are placed in different houses can vary. Each school has a staff member, like Yvette Crespo, who becomes the confidante and nurturer of those having a difficult time. Often that staff "mother" is a woman, but sometimes it's a man who steps forward and takes on that role. One size won't fit all. The point is not simply to have a formula for the staff roles at an Eagle school, but to have staff members who can observe the changing needs of students, who can understand the lives they are living and the challenges they face, and then look for someone in the Eagle family who can help our young men meet those challenges.

As I have shown in the preceding chapters, there are seven areas in a young man's life that will make the difference. Young men need:

Safe passage. No matter where they live, there is going to be physical danger in their environments. As they become teenagers, they will range farther and take more risks, increasingly exposing themselves to those dangers, which might include: physical harm, gang membership and other crime, exposure to alcohol and drugs, premature fatherhood, incarceration, or suicide, among others. Young men need adults to help map out the risks in advance: Where are the trouble spots? They need to learn how to find safe passage around such dangers. That includes a structure for their days that keeps them out of harm's way, techniques for responding to the trouble they can't avoid, and adults who can help them choose safer, more positive activities when they are not at home or at school.

Positive peer influence. Young men are going to be guided by their peers more than at any other time in their lives. No amount of adult discouragement will stop them from valuing the opinions of their peers or from wanting to live up to those standards. We can't pick their friends for them, but we can encourage them to spend their time in situations (schools, after-school programs, local community pro-grams, and family gatherings) where they are likely to pick positively minded peers for themselves—and to model for them the lifelong pleasures of brotherly friendship, loyalty, and healthy competition on the road to a good life.

Security, high expectations, and love. It may sound obvious that young people's success depends on the influence of their parents and teach-ers, but what is not obvious is how that influence must move in two directions at once. Adults must hold the children in their care to high standards of achievement, expecting them to overcome setbacks and to excel not just academically but in their behavior and moral com-mitment, but they must also provide the reliable love and security that helps young people risk failure in order to succeed. It's a double mes-sage, one that a child can feel when, for example, a parent shows up at school, not just because a young person is in trouble or has a special assembly day, but on an ordinary school day. The message says: *You have to do more—and I love you so much that I will be here to support you every day as you work to meet that challenge.*

Teachers ready to teach boys. For our young men to succeed, we need teachers committed not just to teaching their subjects but to teach-ing boys. That means teachers with enough experience with young men's energy and impulsiveness to see the difference between boyish misbehavior that needs to be patiently curbed and serious disruption or violence that requires a more serious response. And while there is a range of needs among different young men, in general they need teachers prepared to keep a clear focus on goals, to give meaningful incentives for each step of the work, to draw on young men's natural competitiveness, to provide enough structure to protect them from distraction, and to help them to see the practical, real-world conse-quences of what they learn.

Mentors to guide the journey. Every young man, no matter how blessed with family, friends, or teachers, needs mentors. Not just distant emblems of success to try to emulate, or helping hands to reach practical goals in school or work, mentors are committed guides who know how to cross the territory separating a young man from where he has the gifts and the talent to go. A successful mentor will have firsthand understanding of the challenges a particular mentee faces in his home environment, and a willingness to explain, patiently, how a man could overcome those challenges and establish himself in the larger world. He provides some missing building blocks as a boy builds himself into the man he was meant to be.

Discipline that is teaching, not punishment. Someone must play the tough one who faces up to a young man. Someone in his life must be able to say, "No, you can't do that," over and over again, when necessary. But the discipline that helps young men succeed is not punishment that breaks their will. It is the setting of clear limits that will reassure an angry, frightened young man that he will not be allowed to rage out of control, doing harm to others and himself. It must be coupled with the loving guidance that shows how to respond more productively to powerful feelings and frightening situations. It is the discipline that shows a young man: *I stand up to you because I care about you. I want the best for you. And I will help you to reach it.*

A head start on the future. If there is one advantage that separates the successful from the disappointments, it is timing: the successful tend to be those who discovered their goals early on, and started working toward success as early as possible. Young men benefit doubly when adults help them get a head start on the future, first because they can start putting their amazing boy-energy toward positive outcomes and because, as young men, they often need a specific goal and clear rewards along the way to motivate their efforts. In order to give young men a head start on their futures, everyone involved needs to become educated to recognize opportunities. This is true of all three kinds of success—academic, character, and career. Young men need someone to make clear to them: *You are the person who can make you succeed and you are the person who can hold you back, so let's look together at how you can make your way.*

That's a substantial list. No parent, no matter how dedicated, can provide it all. To address all seven areas requires not just one committed individual but what Ron Walker calls a conspiracy of care, a group of adults committed to identifying the dangers and maximizing the opportunities in a young man's life.

When a parent comes to me seeking help for his or her son, I say: Start with observation. What do you have? What are you missing? You might pick one of those seven elements as a place to start. Could you find an after-school program where he could meet peers who are on a positive path? Or could you find one man in the community who could be that young man's first mentor? The key question is not only *what don't you have*, but also *who do you have?* Who shares your concerns and hopes for this young man? Perhaps there is another member of the family, or a friend, neighbor, or member of your church who cares for your son, as well. Could the two of you sit down together and talk about how you could help him to shape his life? Maybe one of his teachers would be willing to meet with you. Maybe you could find three or even half a dozen other adults who share your concerns for your son—and your faith in his potential—and you could all have a meal together and talk about how you could help him reshape his future. It doesn't require a lot of people. We got Eagle Academy started with the help of fewer men than Jesus had disciples. I think of this line from scripture: "For where two or three have gathered together in My name, I am there in their midst."

ALL HANDS ON DECK

As you gather your conspiracy of care, you will find that there are few quick fixes. This kind of work requires putting in real time. Those who are helping will need support and encouragement as well. For that reason, every aspect of Eagle's success has grown in the same way: by identifying the needs of our community and then finding strategic partners who can help meet those needs—even as we help to meet theirs. The most important lesson I have to share is that we must continue to expand these circles of community and mutual support. If it takes a village to raise a child, then the only way the child will get raised is if the village recognizes that it will benefit just as much as the child does.

What will make the difference? Leaders willing to sound the alarm: *All hands on deck!* That's a navy term, announcing an emergency so threatening that it will take everyone aboard to meet the crisis. It won't be enough to sound an alarm once—many have to do it, many times. In my experience, there are a lot of people who are good followers. There are parents who will come together for the sake of their children, educators who will join in for the sake of their students, business leaders who will participate for the sake of their customers, their labor supply, and their bottom lines. There are faith leaders who will join for their followers and politicians who will join for their constituents. So many are willing to do the job that's asked of them, but they are waiting for leaders to sound the call to action.

It will take all of us to give every young man the chance to soar to the heights of his abilities, and when they do, together, we will lift this country up with them.

APPENDIX

More on the Founding of the Eagle

START FROM WITHIN

The Reverend Jacques DeGraff, one of the founders of the first Eagle Academy school in 2004, traces the inspiration for our work back to 1995. The Million Man March gathered African-Americans in the nation's capital to show the world a fresh image of what black men could be and do. As Reverend DeGraff describes it, "They made the call for a million men, so I felt I had to be there, but frankly, in my own mind, I went hoping there would be at least a hundred thousand. When we got to the National Mall and we saw a million men, it was a transcendent moment for me. There wasn't any violence. It was so peaceful and moved so smoothly—there was a spirit in the air that I haven't felt before or since. It was divinity. We saw ourselves that day as black men capable of making a difference. And we came back feeling that if we could do this, what else could we do?"

In the African-American community, women have always been out there, standing up for their children. The Eagle movement was launched because a few men said, *You know what? It's time we do our part as well.* Men like One Hundred Black Men vice president Ben Thompson, Fermin Archer, organization president Paul Williams, and others who asked this question: What if black men could stand up on their own and address this problem that most people thought had no solution?

At that time, we were in the same situation faced by people who now come to me today, seeking help with an underachieving young man, school, or neighborhood. We didn't know how to do what we needed to do and we didn't have anyone to help us do it. But we were different in one key way, which was the idea that we had to use our own resources, our own ideas, and the power of our own commitment to make change. Here was a chance to fix what was wrong with our community by drawing on what was right about it.

For decades, the One Hundred had been active in providing scholarships and mentoring to other schools. We had partnered with a high school that was so dysfunctional it was on a state government list to be shut down, bringing in members of our organization as tutors and speakers to help turn the school around. The One Hundred was also a partner with the Bronx School for Law, Government and Justice, the small co-ed high school where I was principal. They were part of the negotiations and planning with the city to provide the school with a new school building, and they ran a speaker series that brought successful professionals to speak about their careers, including Rupert Murdoch and Senator Bill Bradley. These practical experiences working with both a struggling school and a successful school helped us prepare for the bigger task of starting a school from scratch.

I've said that Eagle Academy was founded by the One Hundred Black Men organization, but there weren't really one hundred men doing the work. We began as a committee of seven or eight sitting around a conference table. Seven or eight men volunteering their evenings and weekends, giving up time with their own families and friends because they realized that the cavalry wasn't coming, and that if the education of inner-city males of color, so long neglected, was ever going to change, then a few men of color were going to have to work some long hours and start the ball rolling. We remembered the words of Margaret Mead: "Never doubt that a small group of thoughtful, committed citizens can change the world. Indeed, it is the only thing that ever has."

When the new school committee was formed, our goal at the time was to launch one school starting with one grade, a freshman class of one hundred students. We had no blueprint for a national movement. We had to trust that the recognition for what we were starting and the resources we would need to continue would come. We stepped out on faith.

DECLARE THE MISSION

If you spend any time in the world of education, you will find that there are whole industries of speech-makers and conference-givers who travel the country telling us what's wrong with students of color and with young men overall. They can talk to you all day about the problems with the educational system in general—and often, they are right. But while we have so much talk, we don't have enough people working to make practical change. The kind of partners who will complete a mission are not those who have found a way to make a living by talking endlessly about a problem, but those who feel a calling to get the problem solved. For that reason, it's important to declare the mission to the world.

When we created our New School committee, it sounded like a perfectly good name, but we came to realize that the name didn't show potential partners all we were trying to do. Our calling was not to found a new school, but to create a national legacy of self-empowerment and hope—and founding a school was only one step toward that legacy. So in time we changed the name from the New School committee to the Legacy committee. It was a defining moment for our organization, both in recognizing our purpose and in communicating that purpose to others. Now, when the committee reached out to politicians who would need to approve the school, when we interviewed teachers and administrators to work at the school, and when we recruited the mentors we would need to fulfill our vision of a school with outside mentoring for every student, our clarity helped them understand a little better what we would be asking them to do.

Not everyone working with us shared our calling. Before I was considered for the position of principal, there was another person who had been selected to help bring the first Eagle school into being. However, after we got approval from the Bloomberg administration, our principal-to-be had a change of heart. "I talked to my wife over the weekend," he told me, "and decided I'm not going to move forward. I always wanted to be principal of a little neighborhood school, but this is huge. Nobody's ever done this. We'd be under this spotlight all the time and we will have to navigate all of these politics. I'm not sure I can do all that. I feel like the weight of the race is on me."

I tried to convince him that the situation wasn't really so serious, but he wouldn't be convinced, and in many ways he was right. Founding Eagle Academy was a bigger deal, a more ambitious mission, than I probably allowed myself to admit at the time. We intended to show the world that things could be otherwise for young men, starting with young men of color. We were, in fact, taking some of the weight of the race on our shoulders. As Reverend DeGraff puts it, "After we were gone, as individuals and as an organization, this is what we wanted our legacy to be, the monument to our existence. Our successes would not be measured by our stock portfolios or our closets or what we had in the driveway. Rather, we wanted to be measured by the success of this institution." We aspired to help change the course of our history. We needed to find and partner with those ready to shoulder some of that weight.

ACKNOWLEDGMENTS

I would like to thank my mom and dad, who believed in me, inspired me, and encouraged me throughout my life. I could never thank you enough.

I want to thank my family: Betty, for all of your support throughout the years, and to my children, Jamaal, Aaliyah, Ali, Rashaad, and my granddaughter, Hayleigh—you all have been my greatest joy.

My brothers Philip and Terence—I could not have asked for two better brothers. I love you.

To my grandparents, Grandma Pearl, Banks, Nana and Grandpa Clyde, each of whom gave me the best memories a boy can have.

I'd like to thank all of my extended family, who have always encouraged me and in particular my cousins Rodney Plummer and Nathaniel Cook.

I would like to thank Todd Shuster, my agent, Dawn Davis, my editor, Greg Lichtenberg, my cowriter, Rockelle Henderson, my publicist, as well as Beryl Frishtick and everyone at Simon & Schuster who helped make this book a reality.

I want to thank all of my friends, whom I've known over the years, particularly those growing up on Montgomery Street in Brooklyn and especially 223rd Street in Queens, the best block in the world!

I would like to thank the One Hundred Black Men, Inc., including all of the original "founders" of the Eagle Academy—Paul T. Williams, Fermin Archer, Buddy Johnson, Rev. Jacques A. De-Graff, Jim Harrison, Kevin Jackson, and our honorary One Hundred Brother, Felipe Luciano.

A special note of thanks to Ben Thompson, who was the head of the Legacy Committee, which served as the inspiration, and who did the hard work in creating the Eagle Academy.

I would like to thank our political supporters, who helped to make Eagle Academy a reality, including the Honorable Hillary Rodham Clinton, Honorable Michael Bloomberg, former NYC chancellors Joel Klein and Dennis Walcott.

I would like to thank the Board of Directors, Advisory Board, and Junior Board of the Eagle Academy Foundation, as well as our funders, partners, mentors, and supporters.

A special note of thanks to my "big brother" Ron Walker and my dear friend Shawn Dove, head of the Campaign for Black Male Achievement, for encouraging me to write this book.

Very special thanks to two of my elementary school teachers at PS 161 in Brooklyn: Mrs. Mertz, who wrote a comment on the back of one of my composition papers, "I fully expect to pick up a book one day and it will say, "author, David C. Banks." Well, Mrs. Mertz, here it is! And Mrs. Mildred Scott, who taught lessons in black history that raised my consciousness and inspire me to this day. Thank you and I'll never forget you. Rest in Peace, Mrs. Scott.

I'd like to thank Richard Kahn, who offered me my first principalship at Bronx School for Law, Government and Justice. I thank Meisha Ross-Porter and Brenda Tucker for being two of my dearest colleagues and friends. I learned to be a school leader because of you, and I can't thank you enough.

I would like to thank all of the Eagle Academy principals: Rashad Meade, Jonathan Foy, Kenyatte Reid, Vaughn Thompson, Mahaliel

Bethea, and Osei Owusu-Afriyie, as well as the educators and staff at the Eagle Academy for Young Men. A very special thanks to three people who started with me at Eagle and remain there until this day; Yvette Crespo, Aaron Barnette, and Julia Martinez (the "turtle" lady). Eagle Academy would not have become what it is today without the love, commitment, and the pure dedication that you have given.

I want to thank all of the parents and families with whom I have worked over the years and who entrust their sons to Eagle's care. It has been my honor and privilege to work with you in educating your children.

I would like to thank all the young men of Eagle Academy, who have challenged and inspired me.

Finally, I would like to thank my staff at the Eagle Academy Foundation—Kima V. Reed, Nichele Manning, Donald Ruff, Kristin Pereira, Roger Davila, Susan Waters, Hank Offinger, Jason Forde, and Zach Husser, as well as all of those who have worked with me over the years, including Eagle interns, in addition to Stacie NC Grant, Rovika Rajkishun, Juanita Scarlett, Larry Kopp, Zanetta Adams-Pilgrim, Claire Marx, and Euriphile Joseph.

I hope this book serves as a beacon and a blueprint for all who read it.

INDEX